The Kuwait Fund and the Political Economy of Arab Regional Development

Soliman Demir

The Praeger Special Studies program—utilizing the most modern and efficient book production techniques and a selective worldwide distribution network—makes available to the academic, government, and business communities significant, timely research in U.S. and international economic, social, and political development.

The Kuwait Fund and the Political Economy of Arab Regional Development

PRAEGER SPECIAL STUDIES IN INTERNATIONAL ECONOMICS AND DEVELOPMENT

Praeger Publishers   New York   Washington   London

Library of Congress Cataloging in Publication Data

Demir, Soliman.
  The Kuwait Fund and the political economy of Arab
regional development.

  (Praeger special studies in international economics
and development)
  Bibliography: p.
  Includes index.
  1. al-Sunduq al-Kuwayti lil-Tanmiyah al-Iqtisadiyah
al- Arabiyah. 2. al-Sunduq al- Arabi lil-Inma al-
Iqtisadi wa-al-Ijtima i. 3. Economic assistance,
Kuwaiti—Arab countries. I. Title.
HC498.D42   338,91'17'492705367   75-45305
ISBN 0-275-22980-7

PRAEGER PUBLISHERS
111 Fourth Avenue, New York, N.Y. 10003, U.S.A.

Published in the United States of America in 1976
by Praeger Publishers, Inc.

to those who believe in the indivisible
welfare and common fate of the Arabs

ACKNOWLEDGMENTS

This study was prepared as a Ph.D. dissertation at the University of Pittsburgh. The author has benefited from the help of many in the course of preparing the study. The intellectual debt goes to Professors W. N. Dunn and Richard Cottam, of the University of Pittsburgh. Dr. Dunn's vast knowledge of the field of organization theory and his keen interest in methodological problems of social science research were invaluable for the author who had to struggle for a synthesis in the dialectic of theory and empirical reality. Dr. Cottam's knowledge of the Middle East and both his superb scholarship and humane interest in the problems of the area were alternately insightful and supportive. Mr. Abdelatif Al-Hamd, the Director General of the Kuwait Fund, showed a much appreciated cooperation. Dr. Ibrahim Shihata, the head of the legal department of the Fund, was instrumental in facilitating my research tasks in the Fund. His enlightened understanding of the requirements of empirical research is sincerely acknowledged and appreciated. The Ford Foundation provided financial assistance that made the whole undertaking possible.

There are others who helped with their comments and discussions of the various issues raised in the study. Professors Jerome Wells, Alex Weilenmann, and Egbert deVries commented on the manuscript at various stages of its preparation. Many of the professional staff of the Fund contributed indirectly to the study during frequent informal discussions. Needless to say, the opinions and conclusions of this study are solely the responsibility of the author.

CONTENTS

		Page
ACKNOWLEDGMENTS		vi
LIST OF TABLES, CHARTS, AND FIGURE		ix
INTRODUCTION		x

Chapter

1 THE KUWAIT FUND: ORGANIZATION, OPERATIONS, AND GOALS 1

Historical Background 1
The Origination of the Kuwait Fund 5
Organization of the Kuwait Fund 6
   Internal Organization of the Kuwait Fund 8
   Operations of the Kuwait Fund 10
Kuwait Fund Effectiveness: A Goal Model 13

2 THE KUWAIT FUND IN THE FRAMEWORK OF THE POLITICAL ECONOMY OF WEALTH 18

Politics of the Kuwait Fund 21
Organizational Dynamics 28
   Organizational Doctrine 28
   Decision Making 33
   Expansion and Kuwait Fund Organization 38
Effectiveness and the Strategy of the Actors 41

3 THE KUWAIT FUND IN THE FRAMEWORK OF ARAB REGIONAL DEVELOPMENT 44

Kuwait Fund Development Strategy 45
   Loans and Technical Assistance 46
   Nonlending Activities 56
   The Use of Capital 60
Arab Development Expertise in the Kuwait Fund 63
   Arab Identity and Attitude Toward Political and Economic Unity 64
   Political Ideology 68
   Perceptions of the Development Process 73
The Kuwait Fund and Arab Surplus Capital 79

Chapter   Page

4   INSTITUTIONS OF REGIONAL DEVELOPMENT IN THE
     ARAB WORLD: A POLICY APPRAISAL   83

         The Arab Fund: Organizational Structure and
             Dynamics   84
                 The Management of the Arab Fund   84
                 Internal Organization of the Arab Fund   87
                 Organizational Dynamics in the Arab Fund   91
         The Arab Fund: Policies and Operations   94

5   CONCLUSIONS   98

APPENDIX A   102

APPENDIX B   110

APPENDIX C   113

BIBLIOGRAPHY   132

INDEX   136

ABOUT THE AUTHOR   139

LIST OF TABLES, CHARTS, AND FIGURE

Table	Page
2.1 Distribution of Loans by Country, March 1973	25
2.2 Distribution of Kuwait Fund Loans to Moderate and Radical Arab Countries	26
2.3 Kuwait's Net Official Foreign Assistance 1964/65–1971/72	27
3.1 Distribution of the Kuwait Fund Loans by Sector of the Economy as of March 31, 1973	50
3.2 Balance Sheet of the Kuwait Fund as of March 31, 1973	62
3.3 The Relative Importance of Different Elements in Achieving National Development	75

Chart	
2.1 Thompson's Decision Matrix	35
2.2 Decision-making Contributions of Management and Experts	36

Figure	
4.1 The Arab Fund Organizational Chart (1973)	88

The crisis in development as a concept of national undertaking and an issue of global relevance can only be overshadowed by the need to find a solution. There are many avenues by which to approach developmental problems on the national and the international levels. One such avenue is the regional approach. We are here interested in transnational organizations which engage in regional and supraregional developmental functions.

THE SIGNIFICANCE OF THE STUDY: THEORY AND POLICY

This study has two major concerns: first, it is concerned with the complex aspect of organizational goals and how they relate to policy and performance. In that sense, the study relates to that body of organization theory that deals with relationships between official goals, operative goals, the multiplicity of goals, the relationship between goals and policies, and the organizational goal-policy-decision syndrome.

In the initial stage of this research, the author had in mind a comparative study of transnational financial institutions of Arab regional development which would have included The Kuwait Fund for Arab Economic Development,* the Abu-Dhabi Fund for Arab Economic Development, and the Arab Fund for Economic and Social Development. The first two organizations are national institutions created to handle regional functions of furthering Arab economic cooperation and development.† The third organization is multinational and designed to pursue regional functions similar to those of the other two organizations. As the study developed, it became clear that a comparative approach is not feasible since two of the three organizations do not offer enough ground for a comparative study. Both the Abu-Dhabi Fund, which was established in 1971, and the Arab Fund, which came into existence in 1972, did not offer enough wealth of data over time to warrant a com-

---

*Throughout the study the Kuwait Fund for Arab Economic Development will be referred to sometimes as the Kuwait Fund, and sometimes as the Fund.

†This statement about goals is taken from the legal documents establishing these institutions.

parative study with the Kuwait Fund for Arab Economic Development established in 1962. Since the study included field research, problems of creating research contacts and accessibility of data were also a major deterrent to this author in conducting a comparative study. Therefore, the study will deal principally with the Kuwait Fund, with one chapter dealing with the Arab Fund, not so much for purposes of theoretical comparisons as for the benefit of policy insights in the field of Arab cooperation and development.

The second major concern of this study is policy-oriented. The author is concerned with ways and means to further Arab economic cooperation and integration, which he believes will lead to Arab development. A point of departure in this study is a belief in Arab nationalism. Arab nationalism can be translated into policy decisions that will lead, at this point in historical developments, to more economic cooperation and integration among Arab economies. This author believes that value assumptions of a researcher should be made explicit from the start. In this case, some judgments are made throughout the study which are influenced by our value assumption. It should be made clear, however, that there has been a serious effort made to minimize judgmental statements, and whenever they are made, they are based on evidence.

This study asks certain basic questions about the Kuwait Fund: How and why was it established? What kind of goals (official and otherwise) was it deemed to achieve? Who are the various groups or actors influencing the policy formulation process and the dynamics of goal attainment? What kinds of strategies are exploited by these various groups?

Questions about the effectiveness of the Kuwait Fund are raised in the context of goals and policies of the various groups whose actions are pertinent to the Fund's performance. In that sense there are questions about political effectiveness (when goals are perceived mainly to be political in nature) and questions about organizational effectiveness (when goals are perceived to be organizational in nature). This study points out that the Kuwait Fund has two sets of goals; the first relate to legitimizing the independence of Kuwait as a state in the Arab region, and the second relate to furthering Arab regional development and cooperation. The second set of goals is derivative of the first set. Political effectiveness of the Kuwait Fund is related to the attainment of the first set of goals, while organizational effectiveness is related to the attainment of the second set of goals. Since political and organizational effectiveness are related and intermeshed, effectiveness will be dealt with throughout the study as an integrated phenomenon. We are not separating political effectiveness from organizational effectiveness when we deal with the assessment of the Kuwait Fund's effectiveness.

THE THEORETICAL APPROACH

The literature in organization theory offers many approaches to organizational analysis. A recent survey of such approaches identified four of them: systems theory, contingency theory, action approach, and the goal-oriented approach (Bowey 1972). Other approaches can be added to this listing. Mouzelis identifies a Marxist approach, a human relations approach, and a decision-making approach to organizational analysis (Mouzelis 1969). Some recent contributions use an exchange theory approach to organizational analysis (Ilchman 1971; LaPorte 1971) and others identify a political economy approach to the study of organizations (Wamsley and Zald 1973).

A recent trend toward the use of concepts and the perspective offered by the action approach in organizational studies is gaining ground (Silverman 1970; Bowey 1972). Some proponents of the action approach believe that it avoids the inherent conservative bias of the systems approach (Dawe 1970, p. 208), and that an action frame of reference is not prone to errors of reification associated with systems analyses of organizations (Silverman 1970, p. 50).

In studying the Kuwait Fund as a social system with both implicit and explicit goals, we found the action perspective useful. This perspective can be summarized briefly in three essential principles:

1. Emphasis on action not behavior: sociologists realize that by concentrating on behavior alone they cannot make accurate predictions of the way in which people will respond to one another in an interaction situation (Bowey 1972, p. 118). As long as behavior is not fitted in a pattern of motivated action, it cannot be understood. Observing patterns of physical acts coming from various individuals does not have much significance unless it is related to the meanings they attach to their behavior.

2. Action arises from meanings: action occurs, not as a response to an observable stimulus, but as a product of a "system of expectations." This system of expectations arises out of "the actor's past experiences and (defines) his perception of the probable reaction of others to his act" (Silverman 1970, p. 130). An action thus stems from the goals which an actor is concerned with attaining, his definition of the situation (including the range of alternative actions that he perceives to be available to him), and his choice of a means which is likely to be effective, bearing in mind the likely reactions of others to his act.

3. Meanings are socially maintained and socially changed: The structure of meanings in a society can be viewed in what is known as the common sense view of the world. This nonproblematic view of the world accounts for the continuity and smoothness of interaction. An

individual attaches certain meanings to his actions and the actions of
others. If people respond to his actions in the way he expects, then he
is well satisfied that his actions conveyed the desired message. This
indicates that meanings are socially sustained through their reaffirma-
tion in interaction (Bowey 1972, p. 119). As meanings are socially
sustained, they are also socially changed. This happens when social
roles are handled by the holders of these roles in a manner that tends
to challenge the already existing meanings. If actions of others do not
confirm one's own definition of the situation, a process of redefinition
of the situation takes place (Silverman 1970, p. 138). This indicates
that the structure of meanings in a society is changed through the
process of social interaction in that society.

To apply the action approach in organizational studies a profound
analysis of roles should be made (Bowey 1972, p. 120). One needs to
establish the structure of meanings held by each actor. In the words
of Silverman, "the first task of organizational analysis is . . . to dis-
tinguish the orientations (finite provinces of meaning) of different
members" (1970, p. 150). This involves probing in detail the psychological make-up of various actors, their past experiences, and cogni-
tive influences on them which emanate from the social environment.
To undertake a full-fledged, action-oriented organizational study we
need to undertake psychological testing, in-depth interviewing, and
comprehensive socio-historical analysis of the actors in an organization.

Organizational studies are social and not psychological studies.
The proponents of the action approach acknowledge the limitations of
their approach which is more equipped to deal with micro-phenomena
than with large-scale phenomena (Bowey 1972, p. 125). Some sociologists see in the action approach a clear case of psychologism which is
itself a form of reductionism. This sort of reductionism is an obstacle
to a full understanding of the complexity of social phenomena (Cohen
1968, ch. 1).

For the purposes of our study the action approach presents us
with a useful perspective in viewing organizational goals and in analyzing the impact of various groups of actors on the policies of an
organization. In this study, we view the Kuwait Fund as a social system. We speak about organizational goals of and for the Fund. We are
careful, however, not to indulge in reification. When we deal with the
goals of the Kuwait Fund, we discuss the goals of those groups of actors
which actually influence the policies of the Fund. By differentiating
among the various groups of actors who influence the actual policies
of the Fund, we can arrive empirically at a definition of the organizational goals of the Fund.

Some system theorists come close to an action perspective of
organizations using at the same time a systems concept that preserves

the social entity of an organization. Buckley, for instance, perceives of an organization as a system of meanings and alternative responses to information. These give rise to patterned interactions which are "more or less temporary adjustments always open to redefinition and rearrangement" (Buckley 1967, p. 205). The theoretical approach used in this study is influenced by the perspective of an action viewpoint. Moreover, the conceptual tools of systems approaches are utilized without the shortcomings mentioned earlier.

METHODOLOGY

This is an exploratory study both in terms of objectives and methods (Selltiz et al. 1959, pp. 50-65). The objective of the study is not to test hypotheses derived from organization theory in the area of organizational effectiveness. Rather, the aim of this study is to understand and try to explain the dynamics of a development organization, the Kuwait Fund, which operates in a unique political economy setting. The interaction between political and economic variables is the parameter that defines the goal-policy-decision syndrome for the Fund; we are interested in understanding the political economy matrix that affects the goal structure and policy dynamics of the Kuwait Fund. Throughout the study there has been a question in the author's mind: what role does the Fund play in furthering Arab regional development, and under what conditions this role can be furthered?

To answer this question we use a goal model in studying the Fund as a development organization. This goal model permits us to perceive the developmental role of the Fund in the political economy context of Kuwait.

The research tools used in this study include published and unpublished documents, structured and unstructured interviews, a survey questionnaire, and a Delphi technique. It is important to indicate that while in Kuwait for three months (January to April 1974), the author used a form of participant observation as well, to complement the other methods used. Each of these methods will be discussed briefly:

During the time the researcher was in Kuwait, we had access to published and unpublished documents of the Kuwait Fund. The unpublished documents included the Fund's internal memorandums, project files, country files, and correspondence. In writing this study we used our best judgment in revealing sources of information in a manner which would not violate the confidentiality of the Fund's internal documents.

We found Dexter (1970) helpful in suggesting methods for designing structured interviews and in conducting unstructured interviews.

The structured interviews were limited to four cases: one with a representative of the management, and three with senior staff members in
the Fund. The theme of the structured interviews revolved around
decision making, relations between the senior staff and the management, and relations between senior and junior staff. The unstructured
interviews were conducted with some other senior professionals who
were cooperative with the researcher, and some junior staff. The criteria by which persons were chosen for the structured interviews were
length of association with the Fund; closeness to the decision-center
(specifically, the Director General); and willingness to cooperate with
the researcher.

The survey questionnaire (see Appendix A) was administered to
all professional members of the staff and the management of the Fund.
The questionnaire was administered once without pretesting because
of time limitations. In Chapter 3 we shall discuss in detail the general
reaction to the questionnaire and its results.

In investigating views of the staff regarding the expansion in Kuwait Fund operations a Delphi technique was used (see Appendix B).
Delphi is a method that can be helpful in obtaining consensus of opinion
of a group of experts (Dalkey and Helmer 1963). In order to reach consensus among experts regarding a certain issue, the technique involves
repeated individual questioning of the experts. In our case, this repeated questioning was not feasible and whenever the Delphi exercise
is mentioned, it is referred to as a future-oriented questionnaire. Four
members of the organization participated in the future-oriented questionnaire, including the Director General of the Fund and three senior
professional staff members.

A modified method of participant observation was used to complement the other methods used in this study. The participant observation
that the researcher used included systematic recording of observations
gained from the everyday experience in the Fund. The researcher was
assigned office space and was invited to participate in some meetings.
The participation was, however, limited in the sense that the researcher did not take part in meetings involving policy decisions concerning specific issues.

The plan of this study is as follows: In Chapter 1, we shall describe the Kuwait Fund in terms of organizational structure and operations. This description is based mainly on formal and legal documents.
We also describe a goal model for the study of the Fund. In this goal
model we describe two sets of goals. The first looks at the Fund as a
Kuwaiti institution designed to further Kuwait's interests by legitimizing
its independence as a state in the Arab world. This is dealt with in
Chapter 2. The second set of goals are derivative of the first; they perceive of the Fund as a development organization bent on furthering Arab
regional cooperation and development. The role of the Kuwait Fund in

promoting Arab economic cooperation and development is the subject of Chapter 3. In Chapter 4, we shall discuss the Arab Fund for Economic and Social Development from a policy perspective. The reason for including the Arab Fund is to draw some tentative policy suggestions for those policy makers who share our values of furthering Arab regional cooperation and integration. We conclude with an assessment of Kuwait Fund effectiveness and its role in furthering Arab regional development.

The Kuwait Fund and the Political Economy of Arab Regional Development

THE KUWAIT FUND:
ORGANIZATION, OPERATIONS,
AND GOALS

To investigate the role of the Kuwait Fund in Arab regional development we use a goal model described later in this chapter. To understand that role, however, we need to know the historical development of Kuwait as part of the Gulf area and the Arabian peninsula. In the following, a brief description of that historical development is given. We also describe the origination, organization, and operations of the Kuwait Fund as a prelude to an analysis of the Fund's goals and policies in the context of Arab regional development.

HISTORICAL BACKGROUND

The history of Kuwait, as part of the Arabian peninsula and the Gulf area, is not authoritatively established. Whenever the history of this area is written, a process of constructing history is being done. In order to give the reader a brief historical background on the development of Kuwait as an entity within the domain of the Ottoman empire and under the influence of British existence in the Gulf area, we shall depend on published accounts by western (mainly British) writers such as Dickson (1956), Winder (1965), Freeth (1972), and Winstone and Freeth (1972).

The founding of the original settlement of Kuwait is believed to have taken place around 1710. Winder claims that the exact date of the settlement goes back to the year 1716, when some of the Utb (who are part of the Anazah stock of Northeast Arabia) left central Arabia and traveled to what is now known as Kuwait (Winder 1965, p. 30). The reason for the migration is not established but probably the Banu 'Utb were driven by drought to leave their own lands and move in search of water and pasture. Finding a good supply of water on the southern shore of what is today Kuwait Bay, they settled in the area and gave it the present name, Kuwait. Kuwait, in Arabic, is a diminutive of Kut, which means fortress. The name probably refers to a small fort built to guard the early community that settled there. The migration from Najd to Kuwait included more than one tribe. Al-Sabah, Al-Khalifa, Al-Ghanim, and Al-Mulla are believed to have come in that first migration (Winstone and Freeth 1972, p. 61). From among those tribes, the Al-Sabah branch established themselves as the rulers and they continue to rule to the present day. Al-Khalifa moved down the coast and settled in what is now Bahrain, where they are the ruling family today.

The part where the new colonists settled was doubtless settled by other scattered groups, mainly fishermen. The area which is today Kuwait formed part of the territory controlled by the Hasa, a tribe which dominated northeast Arabia. According to Nutting, the Hasa fell to the Ottoman forces in 1570 (Nutting 1965, p. 212). From the accounts of such historians as Dickson (1956) and Winder (1965), the Ottoman control over this area was precarious. The Turks were more established in Al-Basra which was a Turkish Wilayat "state." When the settlement of the newcomers was, more or less, established, the community sent a delegation to Basra to explain to the Turks that they desired to live peacefully. The leader of this mission was chosen by the community to be its first sheikh (ruler) in 1756 (Winstone and Freeth 1972, p. 62).

The relations between Kuwait and the Ottoman Empire are difficult to describe in exact terms. The same applies to the relationship between Kuwait and Great Britain until 1899. Kuwait was never part of the Turkish Empire in the same sense that Egypt and Iraq were. There was no appointed Turkish Wali in Kuwait from Constantinople. Kuwait had not paid annual tribute to the Turkish treasury as did other Ottoman possessions. Nevertheless, as a great power the Turks had some rights that Kuwait was not to question. When the Turks were attacking the Wahabi forces in central Arabia, Kuwait was used as a stopover in those expeditions in 1798 and 1871 (Winstone and Freeth 1972, p. 68).

In 1892, Mubarak the Great became the Shiekh of Kuwait after getting rid of his two weak half-brothers, Muhammad and Jarah. Mubarak tried to ascertain the independence of Kuwait and the right of the shiekh to collect tribute from the bedouin tribes in Kuwait. He also intended to establish peace and stability in Kuwait. For this, he had to play Great Britain against Turkey. Hoping to establish certain rights for themselves in Kuwait, the Turks in 1897 appointed Mubarak their qaimaqam in Kuwait (Dickson 1956, p. 139). Mubarak would have none of such honor, seeing in the move a plot to get control of his country. When Mubarak reorganized the Kuwait customs and imposed a levy of 5 percent on all imports including those from Turkish ports, the Turks

sent a harbor master and five soldiers from Basra to take control of
the Port in Kuwait, but Mubarak would not let them do that. He approached Great Britain in 1897 and 1898 asking for protection, but the
British did not want to interfere between Turkey and Kuwait (Winstone
and Freeth 1972, p. 71).

The British changed their mind about signing a protection treaty
with Kuwait in 1899. By that year, the implications of the proposed
German railway connecting Constantinople with Baghdad were clear to
the British. Germany was competing with Great Britain over trade and
privileges in the territories of the Ottoman Empire. The dangerous
political implications of the proposed railway from Constantinople to
Baghdad and possibly to the Gulf motivated Great Britain to conclude
a treaty with Kuwait. According to the treaty, Mubarak and his successors were not to alienate any part of his territory without the consent of the British government in return for continuous support by the
British government for Mubarak and his successors to be rulers of
Kuwait (Dickson 1956, p. 137).

The agreement with the British also included provisions to the
effect that Kuwait would not conclude other treaties except with Great
Britain; would not admit foreign agents except with the permission of
the British government; and would not grant sponge or pearl conces-
sions except with British consent (Winstone and Freeth 1972, pp. 71-72).

Great Britain has since played an important role in Kuwait's
political development. Under British protection Kuwait survived the
attacks of the belligerent tribes of central and northeast Arabia. In
October 1920, the Ikhwan, a religious group, with the encouragement
of Ibn Saud (who seized Riadh in 1901 to become the amir of Najd) made
encroachments upon Kuwait. They were repulsed by Salim Al-Sabah
in Jahra (Dickson 1956, pp. 253-55).

The need to fix firm and internationally recognized borders between Kuwait and its powerful neighbors became clear. In 1922 the
Conference of Uqair took place with participants from Iraq, Kuwait,
and Najd (later to become Saudi Arabia). The chairman of the conference was Sir Percy Cox, the British High Commissioner in Baghdad.
Ibn Saud represented Najd and Sabih Beg represented Iraq. Kuwait was
represented by the British Political Agent in Kuwait, Major J. C.
More. Kuwait borders were designated with two neutral zones between
Kuwait and Najd and Iraq. According to Dickson, Sir Percy Cox, in
order to placate the powerful and troublesome Ibn Saud, pushed the
recognized territory of Kuwait back 150 miles in favor of Najd, re-
ducing the territory of Kuwait to an area of 6,000 square miles (Dickson 1956, p. 276). Present day Kuwait consists of a strip of land
measuring 7,400 square miles, including the Kuwait half of the so-
called neutral zone (Winstone and Freeth 1972, p. 12).

The discovery of oil in Kuwait did not change much of the political
relations between Kuwait and her neighbors, or between Kuwait and

Great Britain. The discovery and export of oil had a more dramatic impact on Kuwait's domestic, economic, and political development than on its external political relations. This is especially true of the period between 1931, when oil was first discovered (Winstone and Freeth 1972, p. 164), and 1961 when Kuwait acquired full political independence. Although oil was discovered in 1931, the first oil export from Kuwait took place on June 30, 1946.

We have seen the dominating role Great Britain played in Kuwait's external affairs since 1899. This protective role was essential after the discovery of oil. The various rulers of Kuwait have tended to see in the British influence in the Gulf a moderating and stabilizing force. This view was not shared by all political factions in Kuwait. The pride in Arab nationalism that swept the Arab world after Nasser nationalized the Suez Canal in 1956 and united Egypt and Syria in 1958, was felt in Kuwait as in any other part where Arabs lived, and there are reports of accidents when popular expressions of nationalist feelings in Kuwait were ill-received by the authorities (Freeth 1972, p. 109).

Kuwait independence was signaled in a June 19, 1961 agreement with Great Britain by which Kuwait "assumed full control of its own processes of government and its equality of partnership in the councils of the world" (Winstone and Freeth 1972, p. 210). In contrast to independence movements in other Arab countries, Kuwait independence was not acquired through a militant nationalist movement that forced the British out. Kuwait's becoming politically independent represented both a recognition by the British and the ruling family of the changing circumstances in international relations and a realization of the need for Kuwait to follow suit with other Arab countries in ridding themselves of foreign domination.

Iraq's claim on Kuwait was made a few days after independence in 1961. Six days after Kuwait signed the agreement with Great Britain, Abdul Karim Kassem, President of Iraq, called a press conference at which he declared that Kuwait was an inseparable part of Iraq and that he would demand every inch of its territory (Winstone and Freeth 1972, p. 214).

This act led Great Britain to land 6,000 of its troops in Kuwait in conjunction with the terms of the 1961 agreement in which the British guarantee the integrity of Kuwait's territory. Both Arab conservatives and radicals showed disapproval of Kassem's move. King Saud, King Hussein, and President Nasser sent supporting cables to Kuwait's ruler, though Nasser denounced the landing of British troops in Kuwait. Kuwait proposed that the Arab League should provide a contingent to replace British forces following their withdrawal (Winstone and Freeth 1972, p. 216).

The Iraqi claim on Kuwait did not go beyond verbal statement and some army build-up of no large-scale on the borders (Holden 1966, p. 156). The outcome of the crisis was described by a veteran British correspondent on the Middle East: "It was a traumatic experience for everyone concerned: testing for the British, whose resources proved scarcely equal to the task; chastening for General Kassem, who was scared off; humiliating for most of the other Arab states who saw—not for the first time—an imperial power settling their domestic problems for them; disillusioning for the Kuwaitis, who had hoped to celebrate their independence in a burst of Arab joy and brotherhood; and profoundly frightening for all other Gulf Sheikhdoms." (Holden 1966, pp. 155-56).

THE ORIGINATION OF THE KUWAIT FUND

The need was evident for Kuwait to assert its independence as a sovereign entity in the Arab world. The events that followed within a week of signing the independence agreement with Great Britain showed the vulnerability of Kuwait's newly established identity as a sovereign state in mid-1961. Kuwait sent missions to Western Europe, Asia, and the Arab countries to present its case for independence and joining the United Nations. Upon the return of these missions, the idea of creating a development fund was recommended to Kuwaiti rulers "to show the World and the Arab countries in particular that Kuwait is a responsible member of the international community and ready to use its new wealth to help those in need." (Stephens 1973, p. 46).

It can be established with no doubt that the creation of the Kuwait Fund, which came a few months after Kuwait had acquired sovereign independence on June 19, 1961, was a political act. The term "political" has many meanings but a more common use is the one by Easton (1953) which refers to political as involving "authoritative allocation of values." It was realized by the Kuwaiti rulers that the newly acquired independence must be bolstered by the oil wealth in order to be sustained. There are many ways in which wealth can be used to sustain independence. One of these ways is to establish a vehicle for disbursing economic aid. In the words of an Arab economist who was a main figure behind the concept of the Kuwait Fund "(Kuwait) can justify her survival as a political entity in this age of regional internationalism only by serving effectively and impartially as a distributor of economic aid to her neighbors. Herein lies Kuwait's raison d'etre" (Shehab 1964, p. 474, italics in original).

This view of the political need for the Fund as a concept can only explain the ideational part. When it comes to explaining, in organizational terms, why Kuwait chose the Fund and the way it is organized as a means for giving aid we have to revert to two sources of explanation: One is offered by the Director General of the Fund; it represents the more official governmental view. According to Al-Hamad, the Fund was perceived as a means to achieve "a strong desire (on the part of Kuwaiti Government) that Kuwait money will contribute directly in developing the available productive capabilities in the Arab region" (Al-Hamad 1971, p. 4, my translation). This indicates how the Fund's management perceived the ultimate purpose of the Fund according to the will of the political decision-makers. This statement by the Director General of the Fund connotes a major element in his thinking about the Fund. It will be shown later that Al-Hamad's personality and orientation played an important role in shaping the Kuwait Fund as it stands now.

The other source of explanation could be found in a general phenomenon that characterizes Kuwaitis as individuals and their social outlook. In the words of a long time student of Kuwait economy and society, "Kuwait is internationally minded . . . mercantile-entrepreneurial aptitude mark the Kuwaitis as distinct, . . . from their peninsula neighbors." (El Mallakh 1968, p. 12). This mercantile outlook and the concomitant utilitarian approach to wealth, resources, money, and so on can explain (at least partly), the business-oriented approach to aid-giving that the Kuwait Fund exemplifies. In the area of aid-giving, Kuwait, through the Fund, tries not only to give aid in exchange for political goodwill and support, but also tries to make of aid-giving a business that is financially profitable to the donors and economically beneficial to the recipient. It is significant to notice that through 12 years of operations the Kuwait Fund has not had any default on the payment of its loans and has accrued KD 31,506,818 in reserves, which indicates the accumulation of profits from interests on loans and returns on portfolio investments. In appraising these facts one should take into consideration that the Kuwait Fund does not pay interest on the money it lends since its capital (investable and lendable funds) is acquired through equity transfer from the State budget.

ORGANIZATION OF THE KUWAIT FUND

The law establishing the Fund (Law no. 35 of 1961) was only seven articles in length. It provided for the establishment of the Fund as a public corporation with a declared capital of 50 million Kuwaiti dinars, and endowed with the power to borrow money and issue bonds within the limit of twice the amount of its capital plus its reserves. As we shall see later this power was never exercised. The law was amended three times to authorize an increase in the Fund's capital. The capital was raised to KD 100 million in 1963, to KD 200 million in 1966 and recently to KD 1 billion in 1974.

According to the establishing law, the Fund was to be administered by a board of directors under the chairmanship of the minister of finance who was also authorized to issue a charter of the Fund. The original charter of the Fund was put out by the minister of finance in 1962 and the present charter which included minor changes was put into force on April 14, 1963.* The charter deals in broad terms with the administration, operation, and the budget of the Fund but it leaves many areas for the management to decide on. This aspect of the Fund's operation emphasizes a basic characteristic—the ever increasing role of its management (particularly the role of the director general) (Shihata 1973, p. 7).

The board of directors is the body which is responsible for making the Fund's policy and supervising its technical and administrative organization. The board presently includes eight members. The members of the board are appointed for a term of two years that can be renewed. The director general of the Fund has the right to attend the meetings of the board but does not have the right to vote.

According to the Charter of the Fund, the board of directors has the following functions:

1. consider and decide upon applications for loans and other funds of assistance submitted by the Arab countries;
2. determine the mode of participation in the projects of Arab states;
3. approve the amounts of loans and other kinds of assistance;
4. determine the terms of participation in projects subject to two conditions. 1) that the financing of any project shall not exceed 10 percent of the Fund's capital; 2) the financing of any project shall not exceed 50 percent of the total costs of the project, this limit can be exceeded only in special cases;
5. prescribe the manner for investing funds in such forms as the sale of bonds. The board according to the Charter, has the option to delegate the task of investing the available funds to the director general which has been the case;
6. determine the borrowing to be made by the Fund, its amounts and conditions;
7. lay down the staff regulation and supervise the application of such regulations;
8. approve the budget and the closing accounts of the Fund.

_____

*According to Law no. 25 (1974) the prime minister will issue a new charter for the Fund. Meanwhile the Fund is governed by the present charter. The subsequent description of the Kuwait Fund organization and operation is based on the information I gathered when I was in Kuwait (February-April 1974), and other information provided by Law no. 25 (1974) which was issued in July 1974 and a Fund publication that was put out by the research department in November 1974.

The resolutions of the board of directors, however, are not effective until they are confirmed by the minister of finance. The chairman of the board has the right to appoint the director general and his deputy upon recommendation from the board. The chairman also appoints the experts and the senior members of the staff of the Fund upon the recommendation of the director general.

According to the Charter the director general is responsible for the internal management of the Fund from administrative, financial and technical point of view. He represents the Fund in official dealings with other institutions and courts of law. According to the Charter, the director general has the following functions:

1. the execution of the resolutions of the board of directors;
2. preparation of the proposed administrative budget and its submission to the board of directors;
3. authorizing expenditures within the administrative budget;
4. appointing the staff and employees who are not high in the organization to be appointed by the chairman of the board;
5. receiving application for loans and financial assistance, appraising such applications and submitting them to the board of directors;
6. implementing loan agreements; and
7. carrying out other functions delegated to him by the board of directors.

Internal Organization of the Kuwait Fund

The Fund was internally divided into seven departments—economic, engineering, financial, legal, research, public relations, and the Secretariat. * These departments, however, have no charts designing their responsibilities and exact activities. The management of the Fund resides in the director general, his deputy, and the supervisor of administrative affairs. There are no heads of departments and the decisions on day-to-day activities and the long-term planning both reside with the top management.

The organization of the Fund follows functional lines. The main work of the Fund includes reviewing of loan applications and formation of missions to investigate projects, negotiate loans, and advise the Fund's clients on economic and financial, engineering, and legal matters pertaining to their loan applications. The Fund has a multi-

---

*These departments were later made into five by combining the engineering and economic departments into an operations department (The Kuwait Fund 1974, p. 4).

national staff of high professional quality recruited from all over the
Arab countries. One reason for not having department heads lies in a
peculiar Kuwaiti tradition. Institutions in Kuwait generally do not have
foreigners in a decision position. Most of the expatriate expertise in
Kuwait (and the Fund is no exception) are on advisory capacity, and are
not supposed to have authority of deciding on matters involving commitments on the part of the institution in which they work or on internal
allocation of resources within the institution.

The composition of the technical departments is basically of non-
Kuwaitis. All senior experts in the economic, engineering, legal, and
research department are non-Kuwaitis. This fact has affected the organizational structure of the Fund and its methods of operations.

For one thing, the number of senior experts in the Fund has
always been 10 to 15 highly qualified professionals trained in economics, financial analysis, engineering, and law. As of April 1974,
there were 12 senior experts in the four technical departments—four
Egyptians, three Sudanese, two Palestinians, a Syrian, an Iraqi, and
a Yemeni. There were 15 junior professionals of which only two were
non-Kuwaitis.

This composition of the technical staff has implications for the
organization of work, responsibilities, and the decision process in the
Fund. These will be analyzed in detail in the following chapters. However, from a personnel administration point of view the unique composition of the staff affects personnel policies in more than one way.
First, all of the senior experts are on contract basis. In that sense
they are not permanent employees and the rules applying to them change
from one case to the other depending on the time of joining the Fund and
the specific conditions in the contracts.

Second, the gap between the two tiers of professionals (the senior
expatriate staff and the junior Kuwaiti professionals) is very substantial both in technical skills and in the remuneration they receive for
their work. The senior experts are highly trained with most of them
holding advanced degrees from such institutions as Harvard, the University of California at Berkeley, and Oxford. The young professionals
are usually recent college graduates with no substantial training in the
professions. This sharp distinction in technical skills is reflected on
the remuneration system. The contracted staff members receive high
remuneration with an average of KD 600 tax-free per month (KD= US
$3.4). The junior staff members do not receive anything close to this
remuneration. They are treated the same way as other civil servants
in Kuwait, which means that the average pay for a junior professional
would be KD 90-120 a month. The discrepancy in remuneration is
very obvious. Added to this is the fact that the contracted staff members receive other benefits including free housing, transportation allowance, and medical insurance. The noncontracted staff members
do not get the same treatment since they are subject to the general

civil service laws which are less generous than the terms of contract given to the senior professionals.

This double standard personnel practices have created a problem which the Fund management recognized early during the years of inception. It is clear that contracting means divergences, prejudices, and preferential treatment which can ultimately affect the morale of the senior staff. Also the wide variance between senior professionals and the young staff does not help in creating a professional atmosphere of mutual respect and a sense of a peer group. In 1963 the Fund management suggested the adoption of staff regulations designed specially for the Fund (Shihata 1973, p. 10). The board of directors, which is the ultimate authority on enacting such regulations, preferred to rely on the general civil service law applicable to all public employees in Kuwait. As the Fund's legal advisor noted, "it (is) clear that until the Fund's Board adopts staff regulations specially set for the Fund's personnel, the latter's relationship with the Fund will remain subject to controversy" (Shihata 1973, p. 10).

Operations of the Kuwait Fund

Article 2 of the law establishing the Fund stipulated that "The purpose of the Fund is to assist (Arab States) with loans for the execution of their development programs." This article gives the impression that the administration of loans is the major function of the Fund. Article 3 of the Fund's charter, which describes the function of the board of directors, conferred on it the power to decide upon application for loans and other kinds of assistance, submitted by Arab States.

This gave the Fund the option to get involved in the process of development in the Arab region in forms other than giving loans. As early as 1964, the Fund attempted to finance an economic survey in North Yemen that was not concluded because of internal developments in that country. Although the Fund's operations consist mainly of giving loans to development projects, it has also been involved in technical assistance. Sponsoring research on economic development and problems of development planning and implementation in the Arab region has been among the Fund's activities in the last decade. Also, other kinds of assistance have been given to Arab countries to help them initiate contacts with international development agencies. Such assistance has been given to Yemen and Bahrain. In the context of the Fund's ideological commitments and the present political and social developments in the region, the Fund's nonlending activities are significant. These will be treated in more detail in the following chapters.

Another issue which arises in describing the Fund's operations concerns the recipients of aid. According to the Law establishing the

Fund, the recipient should be "an Arab State," but the Charter mentions "Arab States and Countries." The addition of "Countries" in the Charter could mean that Arab countries which do not have a sovereign status are eligible for aid. In the 1960s this could have meant that the Gulf sheikhdoms that did not acquire independence were eligible for aid. However, there was only one case where the Fund dispensed aid to a nonstate Arab country; a loan was made to Bahrain in 1971 immediately before it acquired independence in the same year. This exception was conceived in terms of expediency and practical considerations which prevailed over the strictly legal interpretation of the law. This one example, however, confirms the rule that the Kuwait Fund is interested in dealing with fully sovereign Arab states.

If Arab "states" are the only possible beneficiaries of the Fund, the question of defining such states becomes a cardinal issue. There are some states that can be considered Arab if the term is stretched ethnically and historically (such as Mauritania and Somalia). An easy definition of the Arab nature of the state from a political point of view is whether it is a member of the Arab League or not. For all practical purposes, the members of the Arab League have been the recipients of the Fund's aid.

Recently (in July 1974) the Fund's law was changed to increase its capital and its domain of operations. Accordingly, all developing countries in Africa, Asia, and Latin America are eligible for the Fund's aid. During the second quarter of 1974 a Fund mission toured African countries to inform them of the new expansion in the Fund's activities and geographical coverage and to solicit loan applications. This new expansion of the Fund's geographical domain and coverage is considered by this writer as indication of the political nature of the Fund. It does not reflect any lack of commitment on the part of Kuwait to the Arab countries and it does not change the fact that the Kuwait Fund has been and will be one of the instruments of Kuwait's Arab policy. It is also reasonable to assume that the expansion in the geographical coverage will not be reflected immediately in the Fund's operations since the demands of such expansion in terms of the availability of capital, and more importantly, the number of staff members needed to handle its responsibility cannot be met adequately at the present.

The legal status of a potential borrower of the Fund's money was raised when some public and private corporations applied for the Fund's loans. A literal interpretation of the law would exclude any such potential borrowers since they do not meet the requirement of statehood. To deal with this legal problem, however, the Fund's legal department concluded that the law and the Charter require two conditions: that the assistance is made to the economy of an Arab State, and that an application for it is submitted by an Arab State which is willing to assume certain obligations vis-a-vis the Fund in relation to the required assistance (Shihata 1973, p. 15). These obligations stipulate that the government will be the final guarantor of the debt, that the relationship between the Fund and the receiving party will be immune to those municipal regulations which might impair the Fund's rights (for example, no foreign exchange restrictions on the Fund's operations; exempt the Fund's assets, property, and income from all taxes or nationalization, confiscation, or seizure; consider the Fund's documents and correspondence as confidential and free from censorship). Thus, the Fund's loans have been dispensed to public corporations. As early as 1964, a loan agreement was signed with the Suez Canal Authority (Egypt), and other loans were also signed with public corporations in the Arab countries (for example, with the National Litani Authority [Lebanon], the Societe Tunisienne d'Electricite at du Gaz [Tunisia], and the Banque Nationale de Developpement Economique [Morocco].

The Fund is supposed to give its assistance in Kuwaiti dinars on the basis of its gold parity (Article 14 of the Charter). If necessary the Fund was authorized to give the assistance in other foreign currency than the Kuwaiti dinar. In such cases, repayment of principal, interest, and charges must be made in the same currency of payment calculated at the gold parity prevailing at the time of signing the loan agreement (Article 16/1 of the Charter). Assistance in the local currency of the recipient is also possible but only "in special cases" and by a two-thirds majority vote by the board of directors (Article 16/2 of the Charter).

In practice, the Fund seldom dispenses its assistance in Kuwaiti dinars since in most cases the borrower is interested in other currencies such as U.S. dollars, French francs, German marks. Such currencies facilitate the payment for equipment bought from these industrialized countries. No local currencies of borrowers were given as part of a Fund's loan. This indicates a policy of not financing local expenditure in the projects the Fund is involved in.

The requirement of the repayment of the Fund loan in the same currency of payment is subject to an important qualification "in the exceptional case of an acute foreign exchange stringency" in the benefiting state. In such case, the Fund's board, by a resolution of a two-thirds majority of its members, can accept repayment in a currency of a third state provided that the money used for that purpose be the proceeds from the borrower's exports to the third state, and that adequate measures be taken to secure the approval of the third state on making payment to the Fund in its own currency (Article 15 of the Charter). It is clear that this arrangement is intentionally complicated in order to make it of almost no practical use, since it does not offer much relaxation in repayment to the borrower in need. The World Bank has given a much more practical and generous arrangement to its borrowers who are facing serious foreign currency stringencies. Article 4.04(c) of the Articles of Agreement of the International Bank for Re-

construction and Development (Mason and Asher 1973, p. 766) provides
that the Bank may accept the repayment of loans in local currency for
a period of three years, and/or may modify the terms of amortization
or extend the life of the loan or both.

The question can be raised: why would the Kuwait Fund, which
is aimed at assisting Arab sister states in promoting development, institute such difficult arrangements for those borrowers who might have
stringent foreign currency situations?

There are many explanations for such policy. One is that Kuwait
has other channels for soft aid (direct grants) which can be dispensed
directly from state reserves. Another is that the Fund was inspired
by such a professional orientation in its methods of operation that the
need for keeping a sound financial situation necessitated such arrangements, especially since most of the potential borrowers might have
reasons to ask for the relaxation in repayment of loans in hard currency. By the early 1960s most of the Arab countries, with the exception of Saudi Arabia and Libya, were facing difficulties concerning their
foreign currency reserves.

The rate of interest that the Fund charges on its loans bas been
subject to specific instructions included in Article 17 of the Charter.
According to the article, "in each loan agreement there shall be added
to the annual interest a service charge at the rate of one half of one
percent to meet administrative and other expenses involved in implementing the agreement." It is significant to note that Article 3 of the
Charter authorized the Fund to provide any kind of assistance. This
has been interpreted by the Fund's legal department to include outright
grants (Shihata 1973, p. 19). It seems that Article 17 was included to
insure that in case the Fund decides on giving a loan, a minimum
charge will be added to the loan principal to account for the administrative expenses of the Fund. Although the more common pattern for the
Fund is to charge 2-4 percent interest on its loans, two loans made to
North Yemen (Wadi Zabid project and Taiz-Turba road project) carried
no interest except the 0.5 percent service charge.

KUWAIT FUND EFFECTIVENESS: A GOAL MODEL

Having given a brief description of the Fund, we are now going
to elaborate on the model for investigating the Fund's effectiveness.

In this study we are asking questions about organizational goals—
how they are perceived, who holds them, why, and how they go about
achieving them? Since the study is concerned with effectiveness, it is
clear that we are investigating goals not only on a micro-level (goals
of individuals or groups inside the organization) but also on a macro-

level (that is, goals that can be ascribed to the organization as a social entity with a task to accomplish). Some who deal with organizations using the action approach would conceive of describing goals of the organization as reification faults.

In Chapter 1 we have shown how theorists have tried to overcome the criticism that their approach cannot handle macro-phenomena since its main concern is the individual and how he acts according to a certain structure of social meanings he holds and certain ends he pursues. As has been pointed out previously, action theorists move from the micro- to the macro-phenomenon when they don't speak of the actors in the individualistic sense of the action of a particular actor. Rather they speak of the system of expectations that is established as the actors pursue their ends in the context of the meanings and symbolic resources which they and other actors have as part of living in a social environment that has a certain structure of meanings they draw upon (Silverman 1970, p. 165).

This is not accepted by other students of organizations who think the action concepts cannot handle large-scale phenomena (Bowey 1972, p. 125). For the purposes of this research, however, the orientation of the action approach is useful in dealing with the multiple goals of the Kuwait Fund. In studying these goals we can speak of four groups or categories of actors who are differentiated on the social map. The first group is made up of the political decision makers and policy arbiters on the societal level. This group is concerned with the general political aim of both the survival of Kuwait as an independent entity in the Arab world and their own welfare as the rulers in such a society where political power is assumed by ascription rather than by competition. This group sets the official goals of the Fund and is the final legitimator of the Fund's existence. This means that this group sets the official goals but also should give its implicit support to the operative goals of the Fund as far as these diverge from, elaborate on, or modify the official goals. This group should approve the tasks of the Fund.

The second group of actors is the top management of the Fund. This group consists of Kuwaitis who are highly trusted by the rulers to run the Fund. Their objective is survival, prestige, and they are influenced by an ideological commitment to certain methods of operation based on efficiency, achievement, and financial soundness. This group plays a very important role in shaping the policies of the Fund. They give their professional orientation to the Fund. For many reasons the Director General of the Fund, Abdelatif Al-Hamad has come to play a very important role in elaborating on the goals set for the Fund by its creators (that is, the first group of actors). Al-Hamad has been the director general of the Fund since 1963. He succeeded two directors of very short-lived directorships. He was with the Fund before becoming its director general, and since he assumed the position none of the management suggestions has been rejected by the board of directors. This is an indication of the degree of trust put in Al-Hamad, and the concomitant wide degree of discretion and power he holds in running the Fund. In discussing this category of actors a major emphasis will be given to the leadership role of Al-Hamad.

The third group of actors include the non-Kuwaiti senior professionals who are Arabs. They enjoy financially very rewarding positions and assume a crucial role in investigating and evaluating loan applications, and other forms of assistance the Fund is involved in. Their aims can range from having a satisfactorily rewarding job materially to serving the cause of Arab nationalism through participating in the development of the Arab economies and raising the standards of living of the people in the various Arab countries. Although this group have different country backgrounds, they share similar professional and educational experiences and, to some extent, a similar political and social philosophy.

The fourth group of actors are the Kuwaiti junior professionals. They do not enjoy the privileged position of the second or the third group of actors. They are not highly rewarded financially and they do not assume much decision-making power, which can substitute for the lack of financial incentives. Many of the members of this group consider their association with the Fund temporary. The end they have in mind is to gain a high quality learning experience or to use the contacts of their association with the Fund in acquiring other more rewarding jobs.

There is a fifth group of actors but we have decided to disregard them here since they do not have much influence on the issues with which this study is concerned. This group is the non-Kuwaiti staff doing jobs that do not require a high degree of professioanl knowledge or experience. They include typists, stenographers, clerks, and so on. This group is different from the other four mentioned above but their work and actions have neither much influence on the Fund's goals (either official or operative), nor their policies or tasks.

The action approach provides a proper focus for the analysis of goals, policies, and the effectiveness of the institution. However, the literature on organizational analysis can provide us with concepts and tools that supplement an action frame of reference and enhance our ability to delve into the issues relevant to an analysis of the Fund's effectiveness. This can be done with the aid of concepts that illuminate the actors' conception of their roles, their involvement in the organization and the various strategies they use to achieve their ends. Such concepts will be drawn from Etzioni's types of involvement (Etzioni 1961) and Thompson's types of decisions (Thompson, Hammond et al. 1959). Other helpful concepts will be used to clarify the strategies of the different actors as these strategies relate to the Fund's goals, policies, and main task.

Since our study is concerned with goals, the concept of effectiveness becomes the logical focus from a policy-oriented view. Effectiveness may be defined as the degree of goal achievement (Price 1968, p. 3). We indicated that in studying the goals of the Fund we will not be confined to an action perspective that does not accept "goals of the organization" since only individuals can have goals. Rather we will accept the notion of organizational goals as the ultimate ends towards which the policies of the organization are directed. This is close to Perrow's definition of operative goals (Perrow 1961).

Mohr in a recent article tried to clarify the concept of organizational goals in order to make them identifiable and measurable. Accepting the statement that organizational goals are usually multiple and that individuals in the organization, or groups, have goals of their own, he tries to differentiate between two aspects involved in the concept of organizational goals. The first is what is organizational, that is, how the goal (or intent) is to be considered on the collective level? The second is what is a goal rather than a sub-goal, function, motive, or activity (Mohr 1973, p. 473). To identify organizational goals, Thompson refers to the goals for the organization held by those in the dominant coalition (Thompson 1967, p. 128). This definition is not helpful because it involves identifying the dominant group within the organization (which is sometimes hard to establish), and then to identify the goals of that group. Nevertheless, we consider the line of thinking that Thompson represents helpful in solving the goal definition problem at least in one sense. It speaks of goals for the organization, which implies that the work or activities of the organization will be directed toward some end. In other words, there is an intent behind the activities that take place in an organization. This intent is not mysteriously found or suddenly realized, but is the rational design of a group or multiple of groups who have enough influence to mold the activities of the organization toward certain ends. What we have to do is to go beyond the concept of a dominant coalition which Thompson proposes, and use the concept of influence and the ability to direct. The difference between the two concepts lies in the possibility that influence comes from more than one source (so there is no need to speak of one dominant coalition). Also the concept of influence will give an indication of the role of external actors in influencing or shaping organizational goals. This is particularly important in our study of the Kuwait Fund since a major group of actors affecting its goals, policies, and directions are external to the organization itself (that is, the political rulers).

It seems to this writer that this approach is also more relevant to the study of organizational goals than that suggested by Mohr. Mohr, after distinguishing between the two aspects of the concept of organizational goal (that is, the organizational aspect which refers to collectivity and the outcome aspect which refers to a goal versus a sub-goal, function, or activity), deals with the goal concept through an aggregation aspect. Since only individuals have goals, then an organizational goal is the goal of the largest number in the organization; ". . . only the individual human members can intend anything. Thus we must aggregate, and it remains only to select a convincing mode of aggregation, such as average intensity, unanimity, or majority opinion" (Mohr 1973, p. 473).

As we explained in the case of the Kuwait Fund, the aggregation method will not lead to the best approximation of organizational goals. The influence of political leaders on shaping the goals cannot be considered through this method of aggregation. Accordingly we will conceive of organizational goals in the sense of the goals for the organization held by those who have influence on the organization. This conceptualization comes close to Perrow's concept of "operative goals." Yet, it goes a little further than what Perrow suggests since it takes into consideration "the ends" of those influential actors who affect the task operations of the organization (that is, affect the actual policies). We think our conceptualization comes closer to a goal model from the perspective of an action frame of reference.

2

THE KUWAIT FUND
IN THE FRAMEWORK
OF THE POLITICAL
ECONOMY OF WEALTH

The Kuwait Fund is, first and foremost, a Kuwaiti institution dedicated to promoting Kuwait's national interests. The major question, to start with, will be the relevance of the Kuwait Fund as the organizational frame for fulfilling such a goal. Discussing a goal model for studying the Fund, we mentioned four groups of actors with certain ends to pursue and certain action patterns resulting from the intermeshing of ends with the structure of social meaning that the actors hold. In discussing the goals of the Fund, we offered the concept of influence as a basic mediating concept between official goals and "operative goals." It is suggested that this concept will solve the dilemma of searching inside the organization for a dominant group of actors which Thompson calls "the dominant coalition" within the organization. Our assumption is that goals of or for the organization can be determined or can be highly influenced by groups outside the organization. These goals must be reflected in the actual operation of the organization. Perrow calls the goals which the organization actually seeks to attain the "operative goals" (Perrow 1961).

In this chapter we are concerned with defining the first set of goals for the Fund. This set of goals is basically determined by a group of actors who are outside the organization. In this case, the political rulers of Kuwait are the actors who originated the Fund. The conception of the Fund might have been determined by some "experts" after reviewing possible means to accomplish the goal which the rulers had decided on. Earlier, we described the attempt by the rulers to find means of legitimizing Kuwait's newly acquired independence in 1961. Missions were sent to various Arab countries and other foreign countries to present Kuwait's case for independence. The establishment of the Kuwait Fund was one of the suggestions made to enhance Kuwait's political clout in Arab politics, by showing the Arab countries that

Kuwait's wealth is to be shared for the benefit of the development of the region. Such a step would insure the political goodwill of Arab countries toward Kuwait.

The Kuwait Fund is, in the first place, an instrument of Kuwait's foreign policy. This fact is reflected in the organization of the Fund and in its decision-making dynamics. The Fund is a Kuwaiti institution designed to achieve goals pertaining to Kuwait's interests within the Arab region. As far as this aspect of the Fund's policies is concerned we can speak of the Kuwaiti characteristics of the Fund, despite the multinational composition of its staff and its announced regional functions with the underlying Pan-Arab ideology behind these functions. There are many institutions geared to promoting regional development in the Arab World. These institutions (such as the Arab League bodies: the council of economic unity, the various Arab specialized agencies interested in economic aspects of cooperation such as confederation of Arab labor unions, and the Arab Fund for Economic and Social Development) are different from the Kuwait Fund both in the hierarchy of goals they pursue and in their authority structures and policy-making processes. In the case of the multinationally controlled institutions the authority and power of the management is inherently constrained by institutional arrangements, which is not the case of the nationally controlled Kuwait Fund. Problems of loyalty and trust are of a different nature in both types of organizations. Although the regionally controlled institutions and the nationally controlled ones have almost identical announced goals (that is, the economic and social development of the Arab countries), they have two different organizational ideologies to pursue the announced goal; it is more significant that the announced goal should not be taken for granted as the supreme "operative goal" for both types of organizations. This chapter deals with the effectiveness of the Kuwait Fund as a national institution that serves regional functions for the sake of promoting the state interests of Kuwait.

In appraising the effectiveness of the Kuwait Fund in terms of meeting its first set of goals (that is, serving Kuwait's interests by promoting political goodwill among Arab regimes toward Kuwait and assuring the legitimacy of Kuwait as an independent state in the Arab community of states), we are in fact dealing with the question of the relevance of such an organizational device as the Kuwait Fund in meeting such goals. In the case of other countries different organizational devices have been used. In the United States, the USAID is doing a similar political task as the Kuwait Fund but with a different organizational structure.

It must be noted that the geographical scope of operations of the Kuwait Fund is relatively limited in comparison with the geographical scope of operations of such other institutions as USAID. This can be one of the reasons why Kuwait opted for such an organizational structure instead of having its aid-giving instrument linked to the Foreign Ministry. However, in a recent governmental decision the scope of the Kuwait Fund was expanded tremendously. According to Law no. 25/1974 regarding the reorganization of the Fund, its scope of operations was expanded to include the Arab states and the developing nations (Article 2) and the declared capital was raised to a billion KD (equivalent to U.S. $3.4 billion).

It is premature to judge whether the Fund in its new expanded role will be as an effective instrument as it was before, but we take the government decision to increase the Fund's capital and scope of operations to be indicative of two things:

One, the Fund is an organizational innovation in the field of foreign aid administration which has been tried and the decision has come to confirm the success of this organizational device as an instrument of aid administration. The Director General of the Fund listed its advantages as an organizational device in foreign aid administration as follows:

> It has made for continuity in the flow of assistance, and relieved the aid administration from going periodically before a not always enthusiastic legislature for new appropriations.

> It has also allowed for the participation of the private as well as the public sector in the enterprise, through a composite board of directors where prominent private citizens share the thinking and the responsibility.

> Incorporation has led to the adoption of a businesslike style, free from routine restrictions and geared to sound financial standards.

> It has also encouraged the recruitment of a multinational staff which in our case has proved to be of distinct advantage. (Al-Hamad 1974, p. 10)

Two, the Fund proved to be highly effective in meeting its goals (we mean here the first set of goals) and this is at least part of the reason why the political decision makers in Kuwait decided on the expansion in its scope of operations. In other words, the organization proved effective in meeting the goals of legitimizing Kuwait's independence and assuring the political goodwill and support of Arab regimes.

In investigating the effectiveness of the Fund to meet this set of goals we will deal with the politics of the Fund, the organizational dynamics in the Fund, and effectiveness as the outcome of group interaction.

POLITICS OF THE KUWAIT FUND

The political aspects of the Fund are very subtle. We noticed that the mere creation of the Fund was a political act and the objective of the Fund is political, but does politics determine the Fund's operations? Does political consideration affect decisions on loans and grants? If so, how much influence do political considerations have vis-a-vis other economic and financial criteria? Is the Fund independent in making its decisions or is it always, or often, subject to interference from the political rulers?

To begin with, the Fund's political nature cannot be denied. The Fund is an institution dispensing aid to other countries with actual purposes that go beyond the apparent purposes of helping the Arab countries to promote their economic development. * We indicated that the actual purposes of the Fund are political in nature. In discussing the motives of rich Western countries behind giving aid to the poor nations in the Third World, David Wall reduces these motives to two, fear and greed (Wall 1973, p. 49). In the case of Kuwait aid to the Arab countries, and (with the new expansion of the Fund) to the Third World, the motives are not exactly the same. At least they do not include greed because Kuwait cannot perform the function of a technologically advanced society interested in the raw materials and the markets that the poor countries would offer to its industry (as is the case with the rich Western nations). Nevertheless, the motive of fear can be true in one sense at least: to justify its independence as a state, Kuwait with its vastly accumulating wealth must show other Arab countries that this wealth is to be shared. If Kuwait did not do that, the legitimacy of its independence would be undermined (Shehab 1964, p. 474). The fear motive is obvious in this case, especially considering that neighbors like Iraq feel that Kuwait should be part of their country, and the motive of the Iraqis is not primarily nationalistic (that is, pan-Arabism), but more economic and political: getting access to Kuwait's oil fields and extending their influence in the Gulf area.

If the political nature of the Fund is intrinsic to its origination, does this mean that politics dominate the operations of the Fund?

To answer the question we must look from different angles to the same phenomenon (namely, the Fund's operations).

The director general of the Fund believes that the Kuwait Fund has always maintained that its approach to aid operations in the Arab countries is "strictly non-political" (Al-Hamad 1974, p. 5). Also, "we are careful to the utmost not to discriminate between Arab countries,

---

*The distinction between apparent and actual purposes of aid-giving is made by David Wall (1973, pp. 34-48).

in dealing with them, because of some aspect that is internal to the country. We do not pay attention to any matter related to the prevailing social system or foreign policy (of that country)" (Al-Hamad 1971, p. 16, my translation). In the same forum Al-Hamad indicated that another main characteristic of the Fund is the high degree of independence in making its decisions regarding evaluations of loan applications and the soundness of projects that are eligible for financing. Al-Hamad mentioned that this independence is intended by the will of the political rulers.

How true are these statements made by Al-Hamad? We can cite some examples that confirm the main characteristic of independence. Early in 1973 a visit to the Gulf States was made by the personal envoy of an Arab president to investigate opportunities for financial cooperation. In Kuwait the envoy contacted the Fund concerning some projects which were already submitted to the Fund for consideration and had been rejected. The envoy was told that the Fund would not reverse its decisions regarding these projects but would look into new opportunities for cooperation. *

After the Civil War in Jordan in 1970-71, when King Hussein's forces crushed the Palestinian commandos in Jordan, Kuwait suspended its subsidy to Jordan which had been in operation since the Khartoum conference in 1967. After the suspension of the subsidy by the Kuwait government, the Fund continued its aid to Jordan by working out a new project to be jointly financed with the World Bank (Stephens 1973, p. 56).

In some cases, however, political considerations come directly into the Funds operations. When Jordan river projects were contemplated by the Arab League, Lebanon submitted an application for a loan (the Meifdoun Dam Project). The Arab League through its "General Authority for Exploration of Jordan River and its Tributaries" had urged the two parties to reach an agreement concerning the financing of the Project. The Fund was advised by the Kuwait Foreign Office to pay special attention to the application for loan in this specific case. As it turned out no agreement was reached on this project but the reasons were not clear. In personal communication I tried to ascertain what happened. I was told that the loan did not get through because of reasons other than the Fund's own will. It seems that Lebanon did not persist in the application and the project was suspended at that time not out of lack of interest on the Fund's part or because of disagreement on the technical feasibility of the Project or the term of lending. In other words it was not a rejection case by the Fund.

Another incident where political considerations played an obvious role in the Fund's operation happened just before Bahrain acquired

---

*The incident taken from the Kuwait Fund files for 1973.

independence. According to the Fund's Law, loans are only given to
sovereign Arab States. However, for political considerations two loans
were given to Bahrain before it acquired independence. In order for
the Fund to do this there must have been political support coming from
political decision-making centers.

It has been noted that the remarkable degree of independence of
the Kuwait Fund can be attributed to the special nature of Kuwait's
political society, and the efforts of its director general (Stephens 1973,
p. 48). It is true that the Fund enjoys a high degree of independence but
it should be remembered that the Fund's establishing law makes the
board of directors, and specifically its chairman, responsible for the
Fund's policies. According to Law no. 35/1961, the chairman of the
board was the minister of finance ex-officio. With the new expansion
in capital and scope of operations, political overseeing became of an
even greater significance from the government's point of view. Accordingly the board of directors according to Law no. 25/1974 is
chaired by the prime minister (who is always the crown prince). This
political control of the Fund leaves no doubt as to its political nature,
but at the same time it explains the degree of independence the Fund
has in its operations. Since high policy can always be checked by the
chairman of the board, there is no need for interference in the Fund's
operations by other organs of the government. It has been the practice
since the Fund's inception until July 1974 that the chairman of the board
is the minister of finance. When this was changed and the chairman of
the board became the prime minister, provisions were made to allow
delegation of authority by the prime minister to his minister of finance
to assume all or some of the powers of the chairman (Article 7, Law
no. 25/1971). The political control on high policy matters can always
be retained in the hands of the prime minister.

The provisions of political control allow for independence in the
operations of the Fund since high policy is already approved. But as
Stephens noticed, the degree of independence the Fund enjoys can be
also attributed to the personality and performance of the director
general. In order to determine this one must look at the interaction
between the management of the Fund and the board of directors.

The board of directors consists of eight members including the
chairman who had been the minister of finance until the recent change
in July 1974. As of April 1974[*] five of the seven members were

_____

*The most recent information regarding the composition of the
board of directors available to me dates to April 1974 when I was in
Kuwait. The recent changes in the composition of the board of directors
that took place since July 1974 when the new law was issued are not included in this analysis. The new law provided for new organization of
the board of directors and probably it meant addition of some new members to the existing board.

businessmen, one was a high government official, and another was the owner of a newspaper (not one of the prominent newspapers in Kuwait). This composition of the board allows the more powerful mercantile class to be represented on the board. With the backing of the business group and with government blessing, Al-Hamad has considerable freedom in managing the Fund.

Reviewing the minutes of the meetings of the board of directors for the past 12 years one comes to the conclusion that the Fund was not only independent in determining its activities and functions, but also that the Fund's management was the major formulator of policies and the actual planner for the Fund. It can always be argued that this is the outcome of the trust put in Al-Hamad by the political rulers.

The board of directors had (as of April 1974) 66 meetings. The meetings were more regular during the first phase of the Fund's operations. When it was clear that irregularity in holding the board's meetings had become a source of nuisance to the board members, a decision was made in 1968 to hold at least four meetings every year. This has been the practice since 1970.

We have not noticed any serious initiatives coming from the board regarding policy or task performance. Most of the decisions of the board were based on recommendations of the Fund's management. All decisions regarding loans made or increases in their amount, change in terms of lending, or in technical assistance were based on recommendations of the Fund's management. From a policy point of view it is obvious that the board does not perform a serious function regarding initiation of policy. It is also obvious that the management has developed a compelling image vis-a-vis the board; consequently, there is no indication that the board performs serious checking or examination of what is presented to the meetings.

To understand this phenomenon we have to consider two aspects that historically characterize the work of the Fund. First, the pattern of noninterference developed since the early days of the Fund's operations because, in terms of competence to handle the technical work of the Fund, the board members do not have the same level of competence and experience that the management has. The management is aided in its preparation of technical recommendations to the board by a competent multinational staff.

Secondly, prestige-wise, the Fund has developed a good image within the Arab financial community and regional and international agencies working in the development field. This image has reflected upon the work of the management and influenced the way the political rulers and the board members perceive the Fund.

If the Fund management enjoys a high degree of independence and freedom in administering the Fund, the question should be asked: Is there a political pattern that can be detected from the Fund's lending operations in the previous years?

TABLE 2.1

Distribution of Loans by Country, March 1973

Country	Amount (in million KD)	Percent
Jordan	10.22	9.9
Bahrain	9.35	9.1
Algeria	10.00	9.7
Sudan	15.34	14.9
Iraq	6.80	6.6
Morocco	10.91	10.6
South Yemen	0.33	0.3
North Yemen	2.509	2.4
Tunisia	14.80	14.1
Syria	7.00	6.8
Lebanon	2.845	2.7
Egypt	13.30	12.9
Total	103.104	100.0

Source: The Kuwait Fund (1973, p. 16).

There are some interesting figures in Table 2.1 which could have some political connotations. For example, Bahrain was given in two years more than was given to Lebanon, Syria, Tunisia, North Yemen or Iraq in loans for 11 years. The country that got the least amount of aid was South Yemen, which is known for its Marxist domestic policies and radical revolutionary tendencies in its foreign policies, especially toward its Gulf neighbors. The immediate neighbors of Kuwait (Iraq and Bahrain) got 15.7 percent of the total amount while a rather remote Arab country, Sudan, with no special political significance got 14.9 percent of the total amount of loans.

Iraq, which is known to have sometimes aggressive policies toward Kuwait, and at one point during the Kassem era prepared for annexing Kuwait, received 6.6 percent of the total loans. That figure does not have any special significance; it is neither the largest nor is it the smallest amount of loans given by the Fund to one of its customer countries.

If we divide Arab countries receiving aid from the Kuwait Fund into two groups, radicals and moderates, * as Table 2.2 indicates, we

*The distinction between a radical and a conservative is made in relation to domestic policies and the general foreign policy orientation

TABLE 2.2

Distribution of Kuwait Fund Loans to Moderate
and Radical Arab Countries

Radicals	Percent	Moderates	Percent
Algeria	9.7	Jordan	9.9
Iraq	6.6	Bahrain	9.1
South Yemen	0.3	Sudan	14.9
Syria	6.8	Morocco	10.6
Egypt	12.9	North Yemen	2.4
		Tunisia	14.1
		Lebanon	2.7
Total	36.3		63.7

Source: Data presented in Table 2.1.

find that the larger share goes to the moderates. No definite conclusion
could be made, however, regarding a preference of the Fund for moderates versus radicals. If we consider that there are two more Arab
countries in the moderate group than in the radical group and that the
moderates as a group receive less than two-thirds of the total aid from
the Fund, then we cannot say that the Fund decisively prefers moderates against radicals. Also some of the radicals (like South Yemen)
receive direct aid from the Kuwait government through the General
Authority for South Arabian and Gulf States, which was established by
Kuwait to help in the development of the Gulf states.

It is difficult to detect any political pattern in Kuwait Fund lending. An observer noted "a relative absence of political discrimination
in the choice of (the Fund's loans') recipients" (White 1974, p. 38).
One of the reasons for this is that Kuwait has other channels where
more direct political aid is given from State reserves. Table 2.3
shows the Kuwait Fund's loan disbursements as part of Kuwait's official
foreign assistance. It is obvious that the Fund does not constitute a
major channel of Kuwait's aid. It should be noted that the figures for
direct government aid contain aid to both Arab and non-Arab countries.

---

of that country. This classification would get the acceptance of most
Arabs. I considered Egypt a radical for two reasons: 1) its radicalness
was not disputed until 1971 and most of the loans to Egypt were given
before 1971; 2) domestic policies in Egypt are still considered radical
compared to those of Jordan, Tunisia, or Morocco.

TABLE 2.3

Kuwait's Net Official Foreign Assistance 1964/65-1971/72

	Direct government aid	Grants	Loans	KFAED disbursements (net)	Total
1964/65	38.1	—	38.2	10.2	48.4
1965/66	40.1	16.7	23.4	7.7	47.8
1966/67	20.8	15.3	5.5	6.0	26.8
1967/68	61.8	65.9	-4.1†	5.2	67.0
1968/69	46.0	49.1	-3.1	6.4	52.4
1969/70	45.9	49.8	-3.3	5.2	51.1
1970/71*	45.3	49.8	-4.5	-0.002	45.3
1971/72*	43.2	50.5	-9.3	3.3	46.5

*Some of the figures for 1970/71 and 1971/72 are estimates
†The minus fugures indicate repayment of loans
Source: Al-Awadi (1971, p. 35) and The Kuwait Fund (1971 and 1972).

In understanding the operations of the Fund from a political point of view one has to consider two elements which are basic to a sound perception of the Fund's politics. The first is the Kuwait Fund's commitment to a high standard of professional performance. There is a definite policy of commitment to sound procedures in investigating loan applications and in appraising development projects. The incident in which the personal envoy of an Arab president was politely advised of the inability of the Fund to change its decisions concerning the financing of certain projects that his country presented, reflects such a commitment to professionalism. In the same vein one should take Al-Hamad's statement about the "non-political" nature of the Fund to mean a certain degree of commitment to professional performance which is enhanced by the high degree of independence that the Fund enjoys.

The second element in understanding the politics of the Fund is that Kuwait found out that it pays politically if the Fund maintains a strong and solid professional image that is not colored by any political leanings. Stephens noted that "although the Fund has given in project loans less than half the amount given by the Kuwait government in 'political' loans, there is growing recognition that the Fund's money has been more effectively spent, even from the point of view of political prestige," (Stephens 1973, p. 55). From an interview with a Fund expert and long time associate of Al-Hamad, we learn that "it is 'political' for the Fund not to be 'political'; the leaders realized that by maintaining integrity in the Fund's operations and decisions regarding loans, a good image of Kuwait and its independence could be more enhanced."

ORGANIZATIONAL DYNAMICS

The Fund was started in 1962 with very few people working in it. The Fund has had a certain image and prestige, since its chairman, the minister of finance and oil, was Sheikh Jaber Al-Ahmad-Al-Jaber Al-Sabah, who was known to be next in line for the crown prince title. The present Director General, Al-Hamad, assumed the position in 1963. For a while, Al-Hamad worked with Jaber Al-Ahmad and it seems that a trust relationship between the two men has developed since those days.

Organizational Doctrine

According to one account (Stephens 1973, p. 49) there were three persons running the Fund in its early years. The director general used to be his own secretary and messenger boy. This attitude distinguishes the Fund from most other Kuwait government organizations. A typical Kuwaiti public organization is overstaffed and the number of office cleaners and "tea" boys is always relatively high in proportion to the number of employees to be served. The organizational doctrine of Al-Hamad is based on a belief in the most efficient use of whatever resources are available. Al-Hamad wrote in 1971 "we are very careful not to slip into bureaucratization . . . this (fault) is easy to commit because we are an agency that offers services to an extended geographical area, the Arab region, that consists of independent entities . . . we are careful to build an organization of a limited size that consists of a few selected Arab citizens . . . in our work quality always supersedes quantity" (Al-Hamad 1971, p. 17). [*]

This basic orientation has identified the Kuwait Fund since its inception. To consider this attitude in the managerial milieu of Kuwait's public service would lead us to appreciate more what it means. It is a safe conclusion to draw that the organizational doctrine of the Fund in Kuwait is unique. The fact that Al-Hamad has been the director general of the Fund since 1963 is a main reason for the continuation of such an organizational doctrine. It is significant that the Fund, with a working capital of 120 million KD in April 1974 of which loan commitments were over 100 million KD, would have only ten senior experts to handle all operations including loans, missions, and investments in portfolio. To understand the elements of this organizational doctrine

---

[*]Translation by the author.

we will discuss recruitment and personnel policies, criteria for internal organization of the Fund, and the role of leadership.

Recruitment and Personnel Policies

Recruitment is one of the most important elements in the Fund's
organizational doctrine. Since the Fund insists on preferring quality
to quantity, it is only natural that recruitment in itself be a top-
management responsibility which has always been undertaken with great
care and caution. It is significant that none of the senior professional
positions in the Fund has been filled through advertising in the newspapers or by similar methods. We indicated that those professionals
who are highly qualified do the main work in the Fund while junior professionals and other personnel play an assisting role.

The recruitment pattern in the Fund reveals three important criteria for choosing a person to fill one of the senior professional positions. The first criterion is personal trust: those who are recruited
are either known directly to the director general or they are personally
recommended by a close associate to the director. Since the Fund must
be sensitive in its operations to the interests of the Kuwait government
and to the political dimensions of its contact with other Arab governments, the element of trust is basic to the recruitment process. The
second criterion is high professional standards and knowledge of the
field of specialization. It is only very important to have professionally
competent staff if the Fund is to do its business with the limited number
of staff that it has. It was indicated earlier that maintaining an image
of high quality professionalism of the Fund was politically desirable.
The third criterion for a staff member is to have personal integrity and
high standards of personal conduct. This might seem of little importance from a Western point of view, especially nowadays where personal styles of living are thought to be a private matter that should not
affect the career life of a person. In the Arab culture, however, the
distinction between personal and professional life is not widely accepted.
The notion that maintaining high moral standards in personal conduct
is important for the Fund's staff is widespread. Issues of trust and
competence can be linked more readily to policy objectives of the Kuwait Fund, but this criterion regarding the moral character of the staff
is more of a cultural nature. It can be valued in the context of an Islamic culture, where both personal and professional life are permeated
by guidelines for conduct coming from the highest religious source, the
Koran.

Recruitment has been one of the major difficulties in view of the
need to maintain a certain organizational doctrine in operation in the
Fund. Meeting the above-mentioned requirements has put a certain
limitation regarding any major expansion in operations. Added to these

requirements, there is a need to balance national representation in the composition of staff of the Fund. There is no definite quota requirement but there is an awareness on the part of Kuwait Fund management that the Arab governments would like to see a more representative staff in the Fund so that a sense of fairness in the treatment of various loan applications can be maintained. Until this moment the Fund has recruited its staff from Egypt, Sudan, Syria, Iraq, Lebanon, and North Yemen. There are some Palestinians as well.

The recruitment aspect of the personnel policies of the Fund has created a problem. In order to recruit such a highly selected staff, the Fund has had to offer enticing financial rewards. The financial obligations that the Fund incurs in order to keep its senior staff is justified by the importance of its work. The case is different where junior staff and other personnel are concerned. They receive financial rewards (salary and other benefits) which are much less than what senior experts receive. Their remuneration is governed by the same laws that govern other government employees, while the senior staff members get what their contracts allow them to get. The discrepancy is sometimes a cause for uneasiness. It is difficult to ascertain how much influence this discrepancy in financial treatment does have on morale, but generally there are no widespread feelings of dissatisfaction on the part of junior staff or other empolyees. At the same time relations among the members of the organization could improve if dual treatment were to disappear. The high rate of turnover among junior staff members could be lowered if they were given more incentive to do their jobs.

Internal Organization

The most recent official description of the internal organization of the Fund refers to the task force approach as the method the Fund uses in its work—which implies "informal collaboration between the various departments" (The Kuwait Fund 1974, p. 4). These departments include the operations department, the finance department, the administrative department, the office of legal advisers, and the research department.

As indicated earlier in Chapter 1, the organizational chart for the Kuwait Fund is most unusual. There are no formal department heads. It is known that most senior members, in some departments, are de facto department heads but this is not true of all departments. Certainly this is not true of the operations department, which is the most important one since it handles most of the technical work on loans and that constitutes the larger portion of the Fund's operations. The operations department is the outcome of the merger of the economic and engineering departments.

The internal organization of the Fund can be considered from one point as being highly centralized since ultimate decisions in each department are taken by the director general and not the senior member or the head of the department. From another angle, the organization is very flexible and conducive to cooperation rather than conflict. The traditional rivalries and competition for prestige or significance, which are more common in modern bureaucracies that engage in highly professional work, is absent. The concept of a task force approach in the Fund's operations has evolved naturally both as a result of distaste for routine on the part of the top management of the Fund and the actual limitation of availability of staff. The limited numbers of available staff are called upon to study loan applications, go on missions to various countries, attend conferences, represent the Fund in professional meetings, and give advice to the management on technical matters when such advice is needed. Under such circumstances the concept of a task force is really a refined description of an ad hoc approach to handling the work as it comes and dealing with the problems as they arise.

It should be emphasized, however, that this was not the only approach available. If the Fund management had a different view of how duties might be divided between departments and how authority should be exercised, the outcome in terms of internal organization would have been different. The present internal organization of the Fund, which its management boasts to be flexible and efficient, is the result of certain attitudes toward organizational values that the management holds. It is not obvious that the task force approach to internal organization was a deliberate strategy designed by the management at the inception of the Fund.

Answering the question of whether this task force approach evolved as an ad hoc response to work problems or was designed from the beginning as the organizational strategy which the management had chosen, is relevant now when the Fund is at a turning point in its development, represented by the Government's decision to expand its operations. If there is an element of deliberate strategy on the part of the management to keep the internal organization flexible and without definite lines of authority or specific responsibilities for each department or individual in it, we doubt the possibility of a true expansion in the Fund to assume the huge responsibilities associated with a billion-KD operations. There is reason to believe that the present internal organization with its flexibility and nondefinitiveness is congruent with the model of the Fund as a family-type enterprise where personal relations and ties are developed to the maximum since they are conducive to more efficient handling of the work requirements. This close personal contact and appreciation of the value of personal relationships reduces tension and promotes professional contact. The fact that competition among the senior professionals is minimized (since there are no formal authority positions to fight over) is a major element in the apparent efficient handling of tasks in the Fund's work.

The Role of Leadership

The role of leadership is of paramount importance in the Kuwait Fund. There is no doubt that the Fund is what it is mainly because of the definite imprint of Al-Hamad's personality and ideas. As a general rule all members of the staff interviewed agreed that the impact of Al-Hamad's personality and ideas on the Fund's organization and policies is of prime significance. Asked whether the Fund would have been the same if other individuals or kinds of persons were in the leadership position, the answer was conclusive that, with a different personality in the position of director general, the Fund would not have been the same. The emphasis goes beyond mere statement of differences between one person or the other in the position of director general; the accent is always on the uniqueness of Al-Hamad's personality and dynamism. Some of the senior staff members indicated that if the director general were someone else "they would never have been here because this place would never have had such prestige and image with another man as its director general."

We quoted Al-Hamad extensively in policy statements because his thinking and the general outlook of his pronounced beliefs are basic to the understanding of what the Fund is and what it will be. In policy matters Al-Hamad has taken many initiatives. It was indicated earlier that the board of directors plays little role in policy design and that most of the management policy recommendations were adopted by the board. The role of Al-Hamad's leadership in the Fund was emphasized by the other functions he used to have until very recently. Al-Hamad was on the board of directors of three Kuwaiti companies; one of these, the Kuwait Investment Company, is of major importance for the Kuwait economy. KIC used to play a leading role in creating investment chances for oil money and in dispensing with government surplus by investing it abroad. Al-Hamad recently declined membership on the board of directors of KIC to devote his time completely to the Fund.

Besides being involved in the investment field and in managing Kuwait's agency for foreign aid, Al-Hamad is involved with other activities that enlarge the image of the Kuwait Fund and provide him, as the director of the Fund, with added political and intellectual clout. He is a member of the board of trustees of the Institute of Palestinian Studies and is always involved in conferences and meetings of a political and intellectual nature related to Arab political development and regional integration. Recently Al-Hamad has been one of the constituent members of the Center for Arab Studies, which is an institute dedicated to the promotion of Arab unity in cultural, social, economic, and political fields. The main function of this institute is to undertake policy research intended to promote Arab unity in the above mentioned fields (As-Siassa, 10 January 1975). In one of the statements about the role of the Fund in the context of Kuwaiti policies toward the Arab cause, he indicated that "we believe the socio-economic underdevelopment in the Arab world cannot be conquered without the collaborated efforts of the Arab nation itself . . . the Kuwait Fund is in fact part of these efforts: Arab money and efforts in the service of a better future for the Arab individual" (Al-Hamad 1971, p. 18, my translation).

Al-Hamad's leadership role is not limited to the policy aspects of the Fund's work but (as most effective leaders) also penetrates the interpersonal aspect of the Fund organizational life. There is wide-spread respect and admiration for his leadership among the staff members. The fact that the Fund is a highly centralized decision unit is made less implausible by the personal traits of its leader. Al-Hamad's style of leadership depends on a high degree of control (via a central-ized decision system), but this control is not demoralizing for the members of the organization as it often is in similar situations.

Decision Making

Decision making in the Kuwait Fund is an interesting phenomenon to study. The structure of authority is highly centralized as we men-tioned before. Despite that, the process of decision making and the categorization of the decision structure according to Thompson's fa-mous decision matrix (Thompson, Hammond et al. 1959) offers an in-teresting case of centralization.

The study of decision making in the Fund is based on interviews with the deputy director general and three of the senior experts who were chosen on the basis of three criteria: the length of their associa-tion with the Fund; their closeness to the center of authority; and their willingness to cooperate with the researcher. Also the author has de-veloped personal views observing the process of decision-making in the Fund during a stay of three months.

The uniqueness of the Kuwaiti situation is one of the reasons for the special type of decision and policy process that take place in the Fund. Most of the government agencies in Kuwait are staffed by non-Kuwaiti experts who perform the necessary professional functions. On the high policy and decision level, Kuwait is well aware of the fact that decision makers cannot make decisions without the ability to penetrate the substance of issues presented for decision. In most cases when decisions involve allocation of resources or financial commitments on the part of the government, those who are authorized to make such decisions are Kuwaiti nationals. The sense of a need to safeguard Kuwait wealth from being squandered or disbursed in an irresponsible way, makes the government reluctant to authorize non-Kuwaitis to make such decisions. The assumption in this case is that Kuwaitis will be more responsible and more cautious in dispensing monies that belong to their government, more so than non-Kuwaitis who might not care about how Kuwaiti wealth is used. This general attitude is reflected in the decision process of the Fund. The experts cannot make any decisions involving financial commitments on the part of the Fund. The experts generally have no right of signature (that is, representing the Fund in its formal dealings with other institutions, Kuwaiti or otherwise).

Aside from this formalistic aspect of the decision-making process, one finds the relationship between the management and the experts, in terms of contributions to decisions, quite flexible. The management recognizes its limitations in not violating the general Kuwaiti attitude against letting non-Kuwaitis decide on committing Kuwaiti money. Consequently, the experts usually cannot decide on matters involving the Fund's financial commitments on the spot, when such decisions are needed (that is, by missions negotiating loans in other countries). Presumedly, the board of directors would not accept such practice if the director let non-Kuwaitis decide on financial commitments. However, when it comes to professional evaluation of projects or loan applications, the management uses a collegial strategy in reaching decisions. The issues are discussed in a meeting where everyone can give his opinion and will be able to defend it. The management participates as an equal in the final process of voting and the decision reflects the collective expertise more than the single opinion of the formal decision maker. Since most of the issues presented for decision fall in this category we can say that the decision-making structure in the Fund falls in Category (2) of Thompson's decision matrix (Chart 2.1).

Most types of decisions in the Kuwait Fund involve professional evaluation of effects of certain operations or developmental activities on the society. In this category fall the lending operations and other technical assistance functions. In dealing with the Fund as an institution working in development lending and development services, one expects most of the decisions to be in either category (2) or (3). The possibility of a policy decision's being in category (3) depends on the degree of value consensus among the people working in the Fund. If value consensus is lacking then decisions involving development preferences or priorities would fall in category (3). We indicated earlier that the Fund is first of all an instrument by which the Kuwait Government administers part of its overall foreign-aid program. In such an institution one would expect a high degree of value consensus as a prerequisite for

CHART 2.1

Thompson's Decision Matrix

Beliefs about Causation	Preferences about Possible Outcomes	
	Agreement	Non-Agreement
Agreement	(1) Computation in bureaucratic structures	(3) Bargaining in representative structures
Nonagreement	(2) Majority judgment in collegial structure	(4) Inspiration in "anomic structure"

Source: Thompson, Hammond et al. (1959, p. 204).

effective functioning. In the case of the Kuwait Fund, value consensus is assured through the delicate process of recruitment and by smothering differences rather than debating ideological attitudes. When decisions involving the assigning of priorities or any related value implications are discussed, value consensus is assumed by the management to be its own. This means that decisions which might fall into category (3) are in fact transformed to category (2). Thompson indicated that the organizational structure most efficient in handling type (2) decisions operates according to rules which

(1) require fidelity to the group's preference hierarchy;
(2) require all members to participate in each decision;
(3) route pertinent information about causation to each member; (4) give each member equal influence over the final choice, and (5) designate as ultimate choice that alternative favored by the largest group of judges—the majority. (Thompson, Hammond et al. 1959, p. 200)

All these requirements seem to be existent in the Fund if we assume value consensus and we have reasons to assume that it exists and that it is represented in the management preference hierarchy. The fact that management tries to conform to rule no. (4) is very significant in relation to the overall effectiveness of the Fund's operations. Adherence to this rule is important in maintaining the Fund's image in the Arab world and among international development agencies as a highly respected professional institution.

In order to illustrate the decision-making process in the Fund, two major policy decisions are examined and a decision on recruitment is also described. In examining the decisions we are looking at the various stages of the decision-making process which include problem identification, policy formation, legitimation, communication, implementation, and evaluation. This decision-making process is tantamount to a policy process. The reason why we are using this categorization of the process is that we are investigating policy decisions which are important for the overall task orientation of the Fund.

Chart 2.2 shows the contribution of the management and the experts to the various stages of the decision. Information needed for this chart was obtained through interviews and reviews of the Fund files concerning the respective issues.

CHART 2.2

Decision-making Contributions of Management and Experts

Decision Stage	Decision 1		Decision 2		Decision 3	
	Management	Experts	Management	Experts	Management	Experts
Problem identification		X	X			X
Policy formation		X	X		X	
Legitimation	X		X		X	
Communication		X	X		X	
Implementation	X	X	X	X	X	
Evaluation	X		X		X	

Decision 1: Giving Loans to Development Banks

This decision came after it had been noted by the Fund that in many cases development banks in the area are financially weak and cannot, with their limited resources, undertake major responsibilities. In their contact with borrowers the experts identified the problem and thought that by lending money to the development banks these banks could do a better job in utilizing it. The low quality of project preparation in the loan applications for the Fund is one reason why the experts thought of initiating a money-lending policy to development banks. The idea was that the development banks in each country can help in preparing and selecting viable projects that are economically sound and relevant to the overall development plan of that country.

Lending to development banks was debated for some time in the Fund. The research department of the Fund undertook a survey study of the industrial development banks in the region in order to familiarize both the Fund and the banks with the work and interests of each other. Also the study was intended to give insights for future cooperative efforts between the banks and the Fund. In initiating this policy and formulating it the experts played an important role and the management only played the role of legitimizer (through its connections with the board of directors).

Decision 2: Cooperation with an Arab Consulting Group

This policy decision is of more than professional importance and significance. ADAR is a consulting firm that consists of a group of Arab professionals (engineers, economists, and financial analysts). The firm was formed a few years ago among Arab residents of the United States. The aim of the group was to help in developing the resources of the Arab world and to use their high quality expertise in helping Arab investors in identifying, preparing, and implementing important development projects. The decision of the Kuwait Fund to cooperate with ADAR and get them to be consultants on the Fund's financed projects was a decision motivated by more than professional reasons. One can perceive political motivations for that decision in the desire to create more links between Arab professionals residing in Europe and America and their national homes. This policy of creating and strengthening the links between Arab citizens abroad and their homeland has been pursued by the management in other circumstances and by using other methods. One example is the role of the Fund in establishing the Arab Fund for Economic and Social Development and in influencing the recruitment policies for the Arab Fund. In both cases the Kuwait Fund management tried to make the establishment of the Arab Fund an occasion for Arab professionals living abroad to join the Fund and contribute to Arab development through their work with the Arab Fund. As we see from Chart 2.2, the involvement of the Fund's management in the ADAR decision is much more obvious and explicit than its involvement in the decision to finance development banks in the Arab world.

Decision 3: Recruiting a Senior Staff

In this decision all the sensitivity of recruiting comes clear in terms of the contributions of both the management and the experts to the various stages of the decision. Only in problem identification did the experts play a role in the decision. They indicated to the management the need to have a new staff member to handle part of the tasks that the Fund is undertaking. It was only in this stage that experts had a role since they were directly involved in the everyday work. It is obvious that the management followed through the various stages of the decision. Even the implementation stage was undertaken by the management. In this specific case Al-Hamad flew to the home country of the prospective staff member and negotiated with him the terms of the contract. The legitimization of the decision came through the approval of the chairman of the board of directors which the management had secured before implementing the decision.

Expansion and Kuwait Fund Organization

At this point we are asking the question: what will happen to the Fund organizational pattern in case of expansion? Or rather we can ask the question: can the Fund, with its present organizational policies and doctrine, expand to handle the tasks that go with a volume of operations of 1 billion KD?

Asking either question depends on how seriously determined we think the Kuwaiti government is to expand the Fund's activities and how much they can pressure its management to expand. We are assuming that the management is satisfied with the present organizational design and methods of operations of the Fund and is most comfortable in handling its tasks with the existent structure. We are also assuming that the present structure will need to be changed if the Fund is to expand in the volume of its operations. The expansion in the scope of operations means a change from small size to a larger size organization. It also means a change from a flexible family-type structure, where interpersonal relations play a significant organizational role, to a bureaucratic organization where rules and regulations play a more significant role in determing organizational behavior than before.

In dealing with the effects of the expansion in volume of operations on the Fund organization we are talking more in terms of possibilities and probabilities rather than definite outcomes. Also we can choose between answering one of the two questions: how could expansion lead to a change in the present organization of the Kuwait Fund; or how could the present organization of the Fund handle expansion and how might it constrain it?

Since the decision to expand the scope of operations of the Fund is a high political decision initiated by the group of actors who belong to the first group influencing its objectives and policies (that is, the political decision makers), then we can assume that there will be definite pressure put on the Kuwait Fund to expand. The management of the Fund will have to respond to this pressure and show its ability to cope with expansion. We can imagine that there are certain elements of the existing organizational doctrine and policies which the management will try to maintain.

The first challenge that expansion presents to the management is in the field of recruitment. The Fund's volume of work would at least triple in order to begin the process of expansion desired by the Kuwait government. The work of the Kuwait Fund has been done until now in a homogeneous cultural and social context, the Arab world. To expand the operations beyond the Arab countries means that new demands should be met in terms of language skills, diplomatic skills, and knowledge and understanding of the new areas where the Fund will be involved. Diversification of staff is only one element in what should be a new approach to recruitment in the Fund. In terms of numbers only, the staff will need to be doubled to tripled in a matter of a few years. It is doubtful whether that many additional staff members could be recruited in the usual manner (that is, initimate knowledge and trust of the prospective staff member by either the Director General or one of his close aides). At one point there must be a more institutionalized process of identifying expertise and interesting prospective staff in joining the Fund. This could be done through advertising the jobs in the media but it could also mean other methods that go beyond the typical personal contact which has been the case until now.

In responding to a question regarding recruitment that was administered in a future-oriented survey to the director general and three experts, there was a consensus for the need of an increase in the staff number and their specialization. Some of the experts thought that this would be emphasized in the recruitment process during the next two years. One of the senior experts close to Al-Hamad said in an interview that he expects the pressure on the management to recruit new staff members to be a reason for change in the recruitment pattern. He indicated that the management might start advertising new jobs. In an interview with the deputy director general the emphasis concerning recruitment was on the already existing methods mentioned earlier. It is probable that these methods will change but the likelihood of a quick change is not very high. The management feels more secure with the present recruitment policies, and in case of expansion the insecurities and uncertainties accompanying the change would be too much to allow another source of insecurity which might result from a change in the recruitment practices. It can be assumed, however, that the expansion in staff could be handled in the immediate future through the old style of recruitment. The need to maintain closely knit interpersonal relations among the staff and the management during the first few years of expansion will result in dependence on the present recruitment practices.

The second obvious element in the organization of the Fund, which would have to be changed in order for it to expand, is the internal

organization. Internal organization of the Fund must be better defined
with responsibilities and task obligations clearly delineated. The means
that the Kuwait Fund will have to be a little more bureaucratic than it
is now in order to handle a more voluminous amount of work. The rationale for defining a structure of responsibilities and authorities is to
enable an increased number of staff members to handle a greater
volume to work. The existing structure lacks a definition of responsibilities and, moreover, it lacks a functional criteria for handling the
work. What used to be the economics department and the engineering
department have been merged recently into the operations department
(The Kuwait Fund 1974, p. 4). This merger is understandable because
the volume of operations is limited and the number of the staff in both
departments was less than ten. In the present situation the emphasis
on the task force approach to the Fund's work as the efficient approach
is justified. With a larger staff and a tripling or quadrupling in the
volume of work, the formation of a task force would have to be based
on a more elaborate internal organization. Such organization can be
based either on functional criteria (that is, economics, finance, and
engineering departments), or sectors (industry, agriculture, transportation and infrastructure, social projects such as education, health,
and so on), or on a geographical basis (Arab Middle East, North Africa,
Asia, sub-Saharan Africa, and so on). The internal organization, no
matter what criteria are chosen, is important since each staff member
will belong to a department where his knowledge and skills will mostly
fit and he can increase his familiarity with problems and issues related
to the work of his department through his continuous association with the
department. If such a staff member were serving in a task force he
would give an input that represented an accumulation of knowledge and
expertise related to a certain type of problem and he could make a
valuable addition that otherwise might not take place. If the present
structure, loose as it is, continues, no staff member will be able to
develop a particular type of familiarity or expertise regarding a geographical area, a sector, or a certain functional aspect of the work of
the Fund. If the Fund is expanding to include all developing countries
as its geographical domain and financing development projects as its
main activity, it is almost inevitable that certain criteria of internal
organizaiton of the staff have to be adopted.

     When the responsibilities are defined according to an adopted
criterion for organization, it follows that authority will also need to
be defined in order for decisions to be implemented in a sufficiently
smooth way. According to the present structure all decisions are made
centrally (that is, in Kuwait, by Al-Hamad) with the exception of a few
unimportant ones. Such highly central authority structure cannot be
efficient in handling a bigger volume of work with an increased number
of decisions to be made every day. In discussing policy decisions we

indicated that they were made according to a collegial structure in which the management played an equal role to that of an expert. This is true in the sense of a decision process but not in the sense of an authority structure since the final decision has to come from Al-Hamad. This might seem contradictory, but it is factual. In those decisions where management is outvoted by the experts, the final decision is based on the majority opinion but is represented to the board of directors as the management's decision. The formal power to make decisions regarding any matter big or small in the Fund rests completely with the management.

When the volume of operations expands to the degree that it is impossible for the Fund to depend solely on a very central structure for decisions, the authority for decision making will have to be delineated and the sensitive issues related to this delineation will have to be tackled. As mentioned earlier, one of the issues concerns a common understanding that the experts are serving in a completely advisory capacity and that they cannot make decisions involving any commitment on the part of the Fund. This would mean that decisions should be taken by Kuwaitis and no leadership position (such as head of department) can be given to a non-Kuwaiti expert since such a position entails decision rights.

One could expect the expansion of the Fund to affect this critical issue of the relationship between experts and the management regarding decision rights of the former. If efficiency is adhered to, as is the case in most choices that the Fund has made until now, the cultural and political barriers to granting decision rights to the experts can be surmounted. If, however, the political risks involved in granting decision rights to non-Kuwaitis are overestimated, the Fund may find itself in the unfavorable position of sacrificing efficiency. In terms of likelihoods it seems that the Fund will eventually give its experts more authority in deciding on loans and financial commitments. This, however, may happen when the problems of overcentralization or poorly made decisions tax heavily the Fund's performance. As for the immediate future the reluctance to grant decision-making powers to non-Kuwaiti experts may continue.

EFFECTIVENESS AND THE STRATEGY OF THE ACTORS

In this final section we are dealing with the interaction between the actors in the Kuwait Fund. We are postulating that the nature of the ends sought by the actors and the strategies they use in achieving their ends are conducive to an effective overall performance of the Fund.

The first group of actors are Fund management personnel who are interested in building a reputable institution to serve the interests of Kuwait and to contribute to Arab development. Their professional involvement in problems of Arab regional development help make them more pan-Arab in their outlook than the average person of the Kuwaiti elite. In order for this group of actors to achieve its ends it would have to secure two things: the political support of the political decision makers, and the full cooperation of the senior professional staff working in the Fund.

Political support of the Fund has always been forthcoming because the political decision makers trust the director general. By maintaining the reputation of the Fund as being a highly competent organization, the Fund management gives the political rulers what they want and gets in return their continued support. The management has been able to secure the full cooperation and dedication of its multinationally recruited senior staff. The staff members are given extremely rewarding material incentives. They also work in a very relaxing professional atmosphere and enjoy personal satisfaction from being associated with such a highly regarded institution as the Kuwait Fund.

Because the means and ends of these different groups of actors coincide and reinforce each other, the Fund has been able to maintain overall effectiveness in performance.

Sources of strain in the pattern of interaction among the different groups of actors in the Fund have not become a real threat to its effectiveness until the present. The strain in the pattern of interaction can come from at least two sources:

First, the young junior Kuwaiti nationals who are part of the professional staff can be a source of disruption in the Fund's work. As we indicated earlier, they as a group are not highly paid and, what might be more important, they face constraints in their ambitions to play a more significant role in decision making. They hold very little power over decisions and if we assume that individuals usually seek power especially when they feel that it is in their right to acquire it, as in the case of this group of actors, then their dissatisfaction and frustrations over not having enough authority can be a source of disruption in the Fund's work.

Second, the senior professional staff could become a source of strain for an overall effective performance of the Fund in two sources: 1) when they seek power over formal decisions and start questioning their mere advisory capacity; 2) when their values conflict with those of the management concerning Arab regional development. We mentioned, in discussing the decision process in the Fund, that value consensus is assumed in the decision process. The values that the Kuwait Fund management holds are supposed to be shared by the experts.

There is the hypothetical situation when value conflict between the
management and at least some of the experts will be so strong that
it cannot be smothered. At this point the smooth interaction between
the actors in the Fund can be jeopardized, to the detriment of its overall effective performance.

THE KUWAIT FUND IN
THE FRAMEWORK
OF ARAB REGIONAL
DEVELOPMENT

According to the stated objectives of the Kuwait Fund, its main task is to further Arab regional development. In actuality, the announced goal of furthering Arab development is derivative of, and subsidiary to, the more important and implicit goal of enhancing the interests of the state of Kuwait.

This conceptualization of the objectives of the Kuwait Fund explains its policies and the course of action it has taken over the years. The Fund's operations witnessed an evident decline from 1967 to 1969, not because the needs of Arab development had suddenly diminished or that they were met by some other means. Rather, the government of Kuwait felt that, both politically and financially, there was no real urgent need to finance development projects through the Fund after it had made commitments in the Khartoum Conference in August 1967 to subsidize the Arab combatants against Israel with KD 100 million every year.

If the regional functions of the Kuwait Fund and its interest in promoting Arab development and economic cooperation are derivative of its main goal as an instrument of Kuwait's foreign policy, we should expect that the government's interest in, and support for the Fund will follow a pattern determined by political considerations.

The degree of support for the Fund will vary according to the political value the Kuwait government attaches to projecting its image as an active promoter of Arab development. This is determined by a complex of elements related to internal political conditions and inter-Arab politics. A major element behind the interest of Kuwait government in Arab regional cooperation and development is the pressure put on it by the more Arab nationalist elements in the political scene such as the movement of the Arab nationalists represented by Dr. Al-Khatib and his colleagues in the National Assembly. There are also some moderately leftist intellectual groups that influence public opinion regarding such matters as Kuwait's aid to other less fortunate Arab states. *

On the inter-Arab political scene, Kuwait maintains an image of political and ideological neutrality (Ismael 1974, p. 107). This image can only reap its benefits (in the form of declared support of all Arab states of Kuwait's independence and sovereignty) if the neutrality position is bolstered by a more pronounced Arab nationalist attitude. The practical form of expressing such a nationalist attitude will be in the form of aid-giving to all Arab countries without discrimination, and the promotion of regional economic cooperation and development. It is a matter of wise choice that Kuwait created the Fund to do such a function. It is also recognized that the choice of Al-Hamad to head the Fund has helped to promote its image as a viable instrument in promoting Arab regional development and cooperation.

This chapter is divided into three parts: The first deals with the development strategy of the Kuwait Fund; the second with the Arab development expertise represented by the Fund's staff members and their role in regional development; the third deals with the effects of the Arab surplus capital (particularly Kuwait's) on the Fund's regional role.

KUWAIT FUND DEVELOPMENT STRATEGY

It is feasible to speak about a development strategy of such a large lending institution as the World Bank. In the case of the Kuwait Fund, it is not easy to speak of a development strategy since both the Fund management and the relatively small amount of loans given do not allow us to do so with a high degree of certainty. In statements of the Fund management (Al-Hamad 1974, p. 7) and in discussions with the director of the research department, there were no claims on their part that they pursue an articulated development strategy with identifiable elements and a justifiable rationale. The amount of loans given is by itself a small fraction in the overall development spending of the region. It will be difficult to use the impact of Fund lending in order to detect a strategy of development that the Fund adheres to. The reason is that the effect of Fund lending is not very significant in terms of influencing the development of a particular country or the region as a whole.

---

*Such groups as "'Al-Istiklal' (Independence) Association" whose activities include public lectures and articles in the newspapers.

It is obvious that with the expansion in the volume of operations of the Fund, the question of strategy will assume importance. When lending operations start to reach such volumes as $3-4 billion, the issue of their effect on the economies of the region will be significant enough to warrant investigation. The position taken here is that although the question of a development strategy has not been very important until now in evaluating the Fund's impact on Arab regional development, it will be soon. The past performance of the Fund could indicate elements of a strategy, and the policy statements by the management could give us clues to what we can consider a development strategy for the Kuwait Fund. We will try to identify the elements of such strategy by studying the Fund's lending activities, nonlending activities, and use of capital.

Loans and Technical Assistance

According to Mikesell, the types of loans used for development purposes are project loans, general purpose loans in support of balance of payments, program loans, loans to intermediate financial institutions, and currency stabilization loans (Midesell 1966, pp. 32-34). Each type of loan has its advantages and shortcomings from the borrower's point of view and from a developmental viewpoint.

The argument between advocates of project lending versus those of program lending is a known part of the arguments on the use and economic relevance of foreign aid. As for the Kuwait Fund, a review of its activities does not show real involvement in other types of loans than project loans. There are many arguments that can be presented by the borrowing countries that might justify their preference for other types of borrowing than project loans. Many of the Arab countries would prefer general purpose loans which can be used in support of balance of payments since they are mostly deficit countries (except those which are oil rich).

For obvious reasons (besides lack of enough funds), the Kuwait Fund has not been involved in general purpose loans. The fact that it only gives project loans cannot be explained entirely by the relatively small volume of lending money available to it. Program lending has merits that might not be alluring to the more cautious financial lender or the skeptic economist.

Program loans usually are meant to "finance import requirements associated with a fairly detailed program of investment that has been reviewed by the lender agency" (Mikesell 1966, p. 33). Such program lending does not appeal to the Kuwait Fund for a number of reasons. The director general has given his reasons which deserve quoting in detail:

First, we simply do not have the resources necessary
to underwrite, even in part, whole development programmes in more than twelve recipient countries. Nor
are we in a position to make contributions geared to the
needs of a whole economy. . . . We neither have the capacity nor the desire to become involved in co-sponsoring
national development plans, especially when the lines are
sometimes blurred between the elaboration of a plan and,
if I may say so, its fabrication. I shall only add to this
that, when the biggest and most experienced bilateral
source of aid, the United States, declares that it will no
longer have country programmes, that it will prefer to
react to recipient's initiatives, and that it intends to rely
on international finance institutions to appraise the overall development prospects of a country, we should, I
feel, be rather ill-advised to enter the ambitious pro-
gramme finance business, even if we had the resources
to do so (Al-Hamad 1974, p. 9).

The declared reasons for Al-Hamad are basically lack of enough
resources. Al-Hamad's reference to the United States is intended to
show that rejection of program lending is not only for lack of funds; the
biggest country in terms of foreign aid, with all the resources available
for aid, refrains from program lending.

There are other reasons for which the Fund refrains from program lending other than lack of resources. The reasons can be understood when we consider the influence of the World Bank on the Fund's
operational policies. Since it started its operations, the Kuwait Fund
has had very close contacts with the World Bank. For the first few
crucial years of its operations, it depended on World Bank experts to
help in designing its operational methods. This was achieved by having
one or two resident Bank experts as consultants. The loan agreements
with the borrowers are still modeled after World Bank agreements. It
is evident that the cautious policy of the Fund in lending has been at
least encouraged (if not designed), through the influence of the World
Bank.

The World Bank is generally known to have cautious lending policies and although it exhorts bilateral aid givers to undertake program
lending, the Bank itself refrains from program lending and concentrates
on project loans. As of June 30, 1971, the World Bank had granted
1,057 loans and credits, of which only 26 were program loans (Mason
and Asher 1973, p. 229). From an economic point of view, project
loans give the lender a total control over the use of his money by the
borrower. If the lender is particular that his money be spent for its
intended purpose, and is worried about the effectiveness of the funds
he disburses in attaining specific economic purposes, project lending

is preferable. As it was noted in regard to project loans, "Variations in the flow of assistance for acceptable projects will reflect actual progress in the implementation of the projects, (while) a country receiving a certain amount of program assistance each year will not be under pressure to formulate and implement projects of highest priority for its development." (Mikesell 1966, p. 121).

The Kuwait Fund prefers to have such control on the disbursement of its loans through project lending for another reason. Since corruption cannot be ruled out as a symptom of economic and social life in the Middle East, a tighter control on the use of funds by the Fund has both economic and political advantages. Economically, the Fund can make sure that the funds are being used in the proper way and that contracts and biddings are made in a way that brings about the most favorable results from the point of view of an efficient use of available funds. Politically the Fund, through tighter control on disbursements, can make sure its money will not be misused to favor some group, or be the cause of embarrassment if it becomes involved in financial improprieties or scandals.

Acknowledging the reasons given by Al-Hamad for the Fund's policy of project loans, it is significant to note that the change of direction in U.S. policies toward project rather than program lending, which he quoted, stems partly from reasons that are not valid in the Fund's case. The lack of interest on the part of the United States in program loans can be explained at least partly in terms of political rather than economic reasons. American attitudes toward involvement in the internal politics of other countries have changed as a consequence of American involvement in Vietnam. American policies of decreasing their involvement in the economic and political affairs of other countries, what some call "neoisolationism," has political reasons and should not be interpreted as a judgment on the relevance of a certain type of development aid such as program lending. In cases where U.S. country programs failed, political reasons come to the fore as major causes for such a failure. In the case of Kuwait, however, charges of being an imperialist power interfering in the economies of other Arab countries for the sake of its capitalist and imperialist exploits would be invalid.

The need for the Fund to review its policies regarding program lending should become more valid with the expansion in lending capacity. This review is particularly needed for economic reasons pertaining to the borrowing countries. The Pearson report has made the case for program lending by stating the following:

> If aid is to be deployed as to maximize its contribution
> to development, there is no a priori case for limiting it
> to project aid . . . (Program) aid may be spent by the

recipient on a more or less restrictive list of eligible
imports, regardless of whether the purpose is to set up
new projects or simply to keep the economy operating.
Besides capital equipment, spare parts, and replacement components, such imports may include raw materials and even consumer's goods . . . (It) makes the task
of managing a strained foreign exchange budget very much
easier than when procurement for each individual development project is covered by special regulations, and it
goes some way to mitigate the worst problems of (project)
tying by facilitating a shift of purchases toward markets
with special price advantage for particular commodities.
(Pearson 1969, p. 178).

In the Arab countries, a good case could be made for program
lending by the regional local institutions. The World Bank has been
accused of putting too much emphasis on traditional methods of project
appraisal (such as rates of return and cost-benefit analysis) so that it
only finances "the cream" projects which are by any means good investment opportunities. In recent years the Bank has tried to
change its emphasis on project lending and tried to take initiatives in
nonproject loans. It also ventured into sectors that were not tradi-
tionally favored when the Bank used a limited approach to project appraisal. The Kuwait Fund is still following the Bank's old approach to
project lending and it can be accused with the same charges, even when
its terms of lending are much softer than those offered by the World
Bank. Arab economies could be helped economically if the Fund were
to take the initiative of program lending on a limited scale and a selective basis. The argument of limited resources is hardly convincing
with the increase in capital and the accumulating surplus of oil revenues. A more serious obstacle to program lending is the lack of staff
and of supporting organizational structure that can promote policies
regarding such a task. The involvement in program lending will be a
test of a more serious commitment on the part of the Fund to a true
regional approach. This could be achieved when an innovative combination of program lending and a regional framework is operationally
developed by the Fund. The director general responded positively to
the following question (which was included in a future-oriented questionnaire): "Would you expect the Fund to work out a regional plan for
the area and begin soliciting loan applications according to this plan
which has been set up on a regional basis?"

We will demonstrate later that the degree of commitment of the
Fund's management to Arab regional development is stronger than that
of an average Kuwaiti elitist. Nevertheless, for this relatively strong
commitment to be translated into operational policies conducive to Arab

regional development, there are two conditions: (1) political support by Kuwait rulers; and (2) the ability to design workable policies regarding heavier involvement in the process of Arab economic development. This latter condition requires an activist approach toward development. Without the existence of an activist approach on the part of the Kuwait Fund, it might find itself "standing in a line of institutions all of which are awaiting for projects which meet broadly similar tests, in an environment of institutional competition, or perhaps duplication, which causes the relatively small local institution to be drawn into, or even actively to seek, a subsidiary role to external agencies such as the World Bank" (White 1974, p. 37).

The evidence of the past ten years supports White's argument. During those years, the Fund concentrated on the project approach, and followed the methods of operation of the World Bank of the early 1960s regarding priorities attached to different projects and methods used in project appraisal.

Table 3.1 shows the distribution of loans by sector of the economy as of March 1973.

TABLE 3.1

Distribution of the Kuwait Fund Loans by Sector of the
Economy as of March 31, 1973
(in million KD)

Sector of Economy	Amount of Loans	Percent
Agriculture	29.075	28.2
Transport and storage	39.984	38.8
Electricity	20.835	20.2
Industry	13.21	12.8
Total	103.104	100.0

Source: The Kuwait Fund (1973, p. 16).

It is evident that there is an emphasis on infrastructure in the total amount of loans. More than 60 percent of the total amount of loans given was for transportation and power projects.

As mentioned before, the management refrains from identifying a strategy in the developmental lending of the Fund. They do not support infrastructure projects vis-a-vis other development projects. Yet, it is obvious that they have some views on what they want to finance and what they do not want to finance. Social overhead projects like education and family-planning projects are not considered by the Fund. They do not want to get involved in this area of developmental activity, not because they were not asked to (there were some loan applications for projects of that nature), but because they do not want to venture into such fields. The justification that with limited resources they cannot afford to stretch their lending too thin to cover all sectors of the economy, is only partly valid. The Fund is only one of the financiers of the power and infrastructure projects which used to get the attention of the World Bank. White's statement about the relatively subsidiary role that a local financial institution might find itself playing if it were to commit itself to traditional sectors of lending and methods of project appraisal, is obviously valid in this case.

The Kuwait Fund has in fact a large opportunity in influencing its clients to promote one type of project vis-a-vis another. A regular method of financing a project by the Fund starts when it receives a list of project ideas sent by a country asking for financing such projects. An initial screening takes place by the management and the staff, and some of the projects get their attention. In most cases, these projects are in the more traditional sectors of infrastructure or industry. Although most of these lists include projects in the social sector of the economy, such projects are usually ignored. In many cases when countries apply for such projects to be financed by the Fund, the answer is in the form of a rejection.

In a sense, the Fund has a developmental strategy concerning project loans which reflects what the World Bank was doing in the early 1960s. It is indicated that such methods of project appraisal used by the World Bank tended to favor infrastructure projects and power projects (Mason and Asher 1973, chap. 8).

Many senior staff members of the Fund recognize the shortcomings that presently exist in the process of project selection. In most cases project selection is undertaken after an initial list of project ideas is presented. Many professionals in the Fund see the lost opportunities involved in the process: the project ideas presented by the countries are not necessarily the most beneficial to the country. Different lists could have been presented if the process of project identification, selection, and preparation had been undertaken with more professional care. What the Fund professionals think is needed is something similar to the developments that took place in the World Bank when the Bank started "to help a potential borrower locate a promising investment, help to prepare a feasible project, and then appraise the result of its own effort" (Mason and Asher 1973, p. 234).

If this development is to be undertaken, the Fund may arrive at a more sound project selection. This is not, however, the only change that needs to be made. An activist approach which resembles what the World Bank does, could improve the present process of project selection. Another, even more important, change that needs to be made is for the Fund to break new ground in regional development lending. It is not enough for the Fund to follow what the World Bank has done, by assuming a more activist approach in project lending. There is still a need to pursue an innovative approach to Arab regional development:

> It would be misleading, in the Arab context, to see the role of a financial institution in promoting closer economic cooperation as consisting only of the identification of in-tegration 'projects' in the narrow sense of the term. . . . It is clear that a conventional approach to project appraisal, focused primarily on rates of return, will not yield a clutch of projects which add up to an integration pro-gramme. At the same time, it is presumably not to be suggested that the institution concerned should consistently go for projects with lower rate of return, on the ground that they contribute to integration. . . . The technical problem in the appraisal of (integration) projects . . . is not that the rate of return has to be lower, but that the larger returns expected lie so far in the future and depend on the fulfillment of such complex conditions that they are difficult to calculate. (White 1974, p. 36).

To fulfill the task of promoting Arab regional development, the Fund needs to innovate its approach in terms of seeking opportunities for promoting regional projects. Of course this would imply changes in the Fund to promote closer cooperation between itself and other Arab financial institutions, and other agencies of Arab economic development (such as the newly vitalized Council on Economic Unity of the Arab League, the Industrial Development Centre for the Arab States [IDCAS] , and the Arab Organization for Management Development).

The innovations which are needed for a more effective handling of tasks of regional development require, as mentioned earlier, two preconditions. The first is related to the aspect of legitimization. For the Fund to undertake such initiatives and to explore real possibilities and opportunities for the integration of Arab economies, the political decision-makers in Kuwait must give their approval. In other words, it must be clear to the political decision makers that such policies and initiatives will serve the interests of Kuwait. Such a condition might exist when Kuwait finds that it is in its own interest as a capital surplus country to invest heavily in the Arab region. Some of the official reac-tion to a possible American military intervention in the oil countries, which was reiterated by high-ranking officials of the Ford Administra-tion during January 1975, seems to encourage policies of heavily con-centrating on the development of the region rather than using oil money to invest in the West. [*]

---

[*]Such suggestions were reported to have been made by the Minis-ter of Oil and Finance in Kuwait (As-Siassa 18-25 January, 1975).

The second precondition for such innovative policies is to intro-
duce structural changes in the Fund itself. Such structural changes
should increase interorganizational cooperation in the community of
institutions working in the field of Arab regional development. The
kind of structural changes needed is dependent on the kind of cooperation that will be most conducive to the enhancement of regional integration. One possible approach will be to institutionalize linkages between
the Kuwait Fund and other institutions working in the field of regional
development by creating field offices in the cities where a cluster of
these institutions exist, such as Cairo and Beirut. Such a structural
change in the Fund would have implications for its decision process
and the degree of control over operations. The management might feel
that the degree of control over the work of field offices does not meet
the minimum degree of control that must characterize a national institution with regional functions such as the Kuwait Fund. It is evident,
then, that a more effective performance of the Kuwait Fund in the context of Arab regional development might be slightly in contradiction
with the nature of the Fund as a national institution geared to the service of the interests of one country in the Arab world.

It is difficult to evaluate the economic impact of the Fund's financed projects on the national economies of the receiving countries,
since these projects constitute a very small percentage of the total
development spending in the countries where the projects are implemented. We can appraise the value of the Fund's lending to each borrower, however, by estimating the aid element in the Fund's loans.
The element of aid implies that the recipient of the loan obtains resources that he might not have been able to obtain if he had applied for
the loan through a normal commercial or financial channel (for example, the private banking institutions in the international capital market). Even if he could obtain such loans from private institutions, the
terms and conditions of the loans would be significantly harder than
those given in the aid loan.

According to Mikesell, "It has been suggested that the element
of 'aid' in public international loans might be calculated by subtracting
from the face value of the loan the discounted value of interest and
amortization provided under the loan agreement, the rate of discount
being determined on the basis of private market conditions, including
allowance for risk" (Mikesell 1966, p. 28).

The element of aid in the Fund projects is substantial, compared
with other aid sources such as the World Bank, the regional banks, or
such bilateral aid agencies as USAID. The interest charged by the Kuwait Fund on its loans averages from 2 to 4 percent, depending on the
sector in which the project is financed and the general economic conditions in the recipient country. The Fund estimates the aid element
in its loans by computing the difference between the face value of the
loan and the present value of the repayments of principal and interest

(at a 10 percent discount rate) expressed as a percentage of the face value. The weighted average for the aid component in the Fund's loans were 48 percent of agriculture loans, 35 percent of power loans, 35 percent of transport and storage loans, and 29 percent of the industry loans (The Kuwait Fund 1974, p. 18). Some examples of the Fund loans demonstrate the variations in interest rates and maturation period. A loan to North Yemen for the Salif Salt Mine project carried 2 percent interest with a four year grace period and a 25 year maturity period (The Kuwait Fund 1973, p. 7). A loan to Bahrain for the Sitra Power and Water project carried 4 percent interest with a four year grace period and a 15 year maturity period (The Kuwait Fund 1973, p. 7). The Zarqa River Irrigation project to Jordan carried 3 percent interest with a four and one-half year grace period and a 20 year maturity period (The Kuwait Fund 1972, p. 8).

Generally speaking, both rates of interest and maturity period for the Fund loans are more favorable to the borrower than those given by either private banking institutions or international and bilateral lending institutions. For example, by the mid 1960s, short-term lending rates prevailing in Arab countries were as follows: Egypt, 6 percent; Iraq, 9-12 percent; Jordan, 7 percent; Lebanon, 5.5 percent; Morocco, 7 percent; Dubai, 8 percent (El-Mallakh 1968, p. 189). These interest rates have gone up in the recent years an average of from 2 to 5 percent, while the interest rates charged by the Fund have not changed since it started its operations in 1962.

The World Bank loans (aside from the International Development Association credits) had interest charges of 7.25 percent per year for most loans given during calendar year 1970 (Mason and Asher 1973, p. 211). The Asian Development Bank had its interest rate fixed by its Articles of Agreement at 6.89 percent and an amortization period ranging from 10 to 20 years (White 1972, p. 64). More recently, the Asian Development Bank raised its interest rate to 7.5 percent to make it competitive with that of the World Bank (Hass 1974, p. 294). The African Development Bank charges an average interest of 7.75 percent on its loans (The African Development Bank 1970, pp. 15-17). The Inter-American Development Bank offers two types of loans: hard loans, which constitute the majority of the Bank's loans and are given from its ordinary capital resources, with interest of 8 percent; and soft loans, which are given from the special funds that the Bank acquires through donations from governments; the interest on these loans averages from 3 to 4 percent (The Inter-American Development Bank 1974, pp. 37-64).

If Kuwait Fund loans carry more favorable terms than those of most similar aid institutions, there is another aspect of the loans that makes them more advantageous to the recipient country than most of the loans given by bilateral aid agencies. Most of the loans given by

bilateral aid agencies (for example, USAID) are "tied" in the sense that
they require the borrower to use the loan in buying goods and services
in the lending country. Kuwait Fund loans are not tied loans in that
sense. In fact, the Fund makes every possible effort to ensure that its
loans will be used freely by the borrower to acquire the goods and services needed on the best available terms in the international markets.

In the field of technical assistance the Fund is doing an important
job for its clients. Four categories of technical assistance can be distinguished in the case of a development lending institution:

> (a) technical assistance that is not connected with an im-
> mediate investment project—for example, technical as-
> sistance to a ministry to improve its general functioning;
> (b) technical assistance related to the preinvestment stage
> of an investment project of program—for example, as-
> sistance in project identification or project preparation,
> feasibility studies, and sector studies; (c) technical as-
> sistance that is connected with a specific loan or credit
> and is identifiable as a type of technical assistance—for
> example, inclusion in a loan of funds for the employment
> of foreign consultants to help launch the project, and (d)
> technical assistance that is inextricably interwoven with
> the making or supervising of a loan. (Mason and Asher
> 1973, pp. 265-66).

The Kuwait Fund has been involved in these four types of technical assistance. The fourth type (d) has been given special attention by
the Fund simply because of the special type of relationship that exists
between the borrower (an Arab country) and the lender which is also
an Arab institution. In the Fund-financed projects, the borrower
country, in most cases, depends on an external foreign party for either
technical assistance or for funds. It happens that, in most cases, for
a project to be implemented there is a tripartite relationship involving
the Fund, the borrower country, and the foreign (non-Arab) party which
might be a technical consultant or another lending agency (for example,
the World Bank, or USAID). The director general has explained the
importance of type (d) technical assistance in the Fund's operations
as follows:

> We can venture the generalization that unless great care
> is taken [in the Fund financed projects] , things could
> consistently run against the [borrowing] country's inter-
> est. This applied particularly perhaps to the relationship
> with the external parties involved: from preliminary ne-
> gotiations to the delivery of the end product, whatever its

nature, be it a documentary credit, a machine paid for
through a supplier's credit, or a man-month of foreign
expertise. Problems can and do in fact arise literally
at each step, and being able to cope and exercise coun-
tervailing power . . . vis-a-vis the foreign partners
often faces the country with exacting challenges. An
intervention from the Fund at the right time and with
appropriate impact can possibly not only safeguard scarce
resources, but also avoid some eventually unpleasant
surprises. (Al-Hamad 1974, pp. 12-13).

The image of the Fund as a highly professional institution
equipped with exceptionally qualified Arab staff is an important element
in the Fund's relationship with its borrowers and with other international and foreign institutions. The Fund has the technical capability
to deal on a par with the international agencies and to use its own good
image in the regional and international financial communities for the
service of its clients. From this viewpoint, the Fund renders an important needed service to those Arab countries which lack the experience and expertise in dealing with foreign and international agencies
working in the field of development.

Nonlending Activities

The Fund's unique characteristic among Arab organizations as
an institution qualified to deal with the technically complex problems
of development makes its nonlending activities of great value both to
Kuwait and to other Arab countries. *
The Fund does an important job as an adviser to the Kuwaiti
government on various aspects of development services. The Fund
was called upon by the government to give technical advice on establishing an industrial development bank in Kuwait. In most of the meetings that involve development aid to other countries, the director
general of the Fund is part of the official Kuwaiti delegation. These
meetings are very frequent since most official vistors to Kuwait touch
upon issues of aid in their discussions with the Kuwaiti leaders. This
involvement with the general aid policies of Kuwaiti government is more

---

*Some writers use the term "nonlending" to indicate activities
that started as a lending operation but failed to materialize for one
reason or another (Mason and Asher 1973, pp. 169-76). Obviously, we
use the term in a different way.

intense now since the expansion in the Fund's scope of operations to include more than the Arab countries.

In other instances, the Fund has entered into the field of negotiating reciprocal trade agreements. The Kuwait Fund acted as an intermediary between Kuwait and Sudan in an agreement under which the former is to supply the latter with fertilizer in exchange for livestock (White 1974, p. 43).

The Kuwait Fund also played an intermediary role between Algeria and its potential suppliers of funds when it supported an Algerian bond issue. This mediation role became of greater importance when the Fund used its good offices and image in international diplomacy in helping Bahrain to get access to the International Monetary Fund and the World Bank. This last case is of particular importance in the context of the Fund's role as an instrument of the Kuwaiti government's Arab policy. By helping Bahrain in its international diplomatic efforts, the Fund enhances the image of Kuwait as a leading state in the Arab Gulf area.

The Fund's technical assistance effort is especially valuable in the context of nonlending activities. It was indicated before that the technical assistance activities of the Fund included both types: those associated with an investment undertaking (such as preinvestment surveys that lead later to direct investments in the form of loans), and those which are not related to direct investments. The Fund has been supporting a resident technical assistance mission in North Yemen jointly with the World Bank (Mason and Asher 1973, p. 309). This resident mission, which was initially to last for two years, was allowed to continue for another two years when the Fund and the World Bank agreed to continue financing the mission. *

The Kuwait Fund is also sometimes approached by Arab countries to give advice on technical matters such as the establishment of local development banks. The Fund has helped in establishing a tourist and industrial development bank in Lebanon. The Fund's research department made a survey of existing tourist and industrial development institutions and produced a well-defined scheme for a tourist and industrial bank which was presented to the Lebanese government.

The most important initiative, however, was on the collective level of Arab regional cooperation. The Kuwait Fund was a major force behind establishing two important financial regional institutions, the Arab Fund for Economic and Social Development and the Inter-Arab Investment Guarantee Corporation.

---

*The initial agreement between the Kuwait Fund and the Bank in 1972 was for two years. This agreement was renewed in 1973 to have the mission operating in Yemen until 1975.

For the establishment of the Arab Fund for Economic and Social Development, the Fund acted as a midwife. It was on a proposal from the Fund and on the basis of a preliminary draft submitted by the Fund that the Kuwaiti government first suggested the establishment of the Arab Fund at a conference of Arab finance ministers held in Baghdad in August 1967. The Fund has tried, through the Kuwaiti government, to influence the Arab countries to adopt the draft it proposed to the meeting. The final agreement which the Arab governments adopted in May 1968, however, was different from that presented by the Fund (the Arab Fund 1972). The 1968 Arab Fund's Agreement reflects the thinking of the Economic Council of the Arab League in the mid-1950s, which, in 1957, proposed an Arab Financial Corporation; the articles of this 1957 proposal were almost a copy of some World Bank Articles of Agreement. The Kuwait Fund proposal asked for more flexibility in operations and more generous contributions by the members to the capital of the Arab Fund. As Al-Hamad put it, "Our opinion in the Kuwait Fund is that what was appropriate in the forties on a world scale does not seem to be in many respects the best alternative a quarter of a century later for a region like the Arab World" (Al-Hamad 1972, p. 3).

The Kuwait Fund helped the Arab Fund for Economic and Social Development (AFESD) in its early working phase by giving it its first president, who was a former deputy director general in the Kuwait Fund. Also, the Fund provided temporary office space for the Arab Fund during the initial phase.

The Inter-Arab Investment Guarantee Corporation is another initiative of the Fund on the regional financial level. The interest of the Fund in promoting a scheme for guaranteeing Arab investments in the Arab countries was in compliance with Kuwaiti official policies (Shihata 1974a, p. 10). The Fund first proposed three complimentary agreements that were needed to encourage inter-Arab investments. The first concerned objective rules of investment (for example, how Arab investments should be treated by the recipient country in terms of taxation on profits or the transfer of profits to the investor's country). The second concerned methods of settling the disputes that arise in the investment process by stipulating procedures for conciliation and arbitration of such disputes. The third concerned a program for guaranteeing the investments, which the investor might consider a last resort when he feels that his investment is not well enough protected by the two former agreements. Later on, the Fund realized the difficulties that might arise if the three agreements were linked together in one document. Some of the Arab countries might find the stipulation of the first and second agreements not appropriate for them to abide by, despite their interest in and acceptance of the rules of guaranteeing investments made in their countries. The Fund took the practical

approach by designing the articles of the agreement to include only the
guarantee of the investments aspects (Shihata 1974a, p. 11).

The purpose of the finally adopted document of the Inter-Arab
Investment Guarantee Corporation is to cover the Arab investor against

> the risk of expropriation, nationalization, sequestration,
> and other similar measures which deprive the investor of
> substantial rights over his property; the risk for the in-
> vestor of being unable to transfer his income, capital
> amortization installments or debt repayments out of the
> host country as a result of additional exchange control re-
> strictions; and lastly, the risk of material damages due
> to war, military operations, insurrections, civil disturb-
> ances, . . . (Al-Hamad 1972, p. 4).

The agreement establishing the Inter-Arab Investment Corporation was approved by 14 Arab states, and 12 of those ratified the agreement making it effective. In April 1974, there were indications that
the first meeting of the board of the newly established Corporation was
to be held in Kuwait in May 1974.

The Fund has also been interested in building other institutions
that could promote regional cooperation and development in the Arab
region. One of the proposed projects of the Fund is to train Arab
lawyers on legal aspects of international economic transactions with
particular emphasis on international investments and assistance; the
"Law and Development Center" is still in the study phase.

Another institution which is in the perception and study phase is
an "Arab Economic Integration Research Institute." Such an institute
would devote its effort to investigating real possibilities of Arab regional or subregional integration; it would study the various problems
raised by economic integration and identify and prepare specific integration projects.

Building up institutions of regional cooperation and development
is considered to be an important task. In the words of the Fund's director general,

> The fundamental hope we entertain by addressing ourselves
> to the problem of building up (regional institutions) . . . is
> to be able—ultimately and within the limits of our capacity—
> to strengthen [the institutional and administrative web of
> Arab economic life] , to weave some stronger knots into it,
> and eventually perhaps begin to give the whole contexture
> a hue more appropriate to what the modernization of our
> nations really requires. This in my opinion is incompara-
> bly more important in the long run than whatever physical

structures we may be able to help in erecting by financing productive or infrastructure works. (Al-Hamad 1972, p. 9).

Al-Hamad's statement indicates that the Fund perceives its role in larger terms than just identifying and financing development projects. The Fund has sponsored research that aims at identifying problems, conditions, and prospects of economic and social development in the Arab world. In 1968, the Fund commissioned a well known Arab economist of Palestinian origin to undertake a $70,000 study on "Determinants of Economic Development in the Arab World." By mid-1974, the study was in the final stages and to be published shortly. Another more recent research undertaking of the Fund started in the last part of 1973, concentrating on the development planning process in the Arab countries in order to identify obstacles and see how the Fund could contribute to a better planning performance in the Arab countries.

The Use of Capital

The Kuwait Fund has a unique status compared with similar national aid agencies such as USAID, or with regional development banks such as the Inter-American Development Bank, the African Development Bank, or the Asian Development Bank.

Unlike USAID, the Fund has an independent status in the governmental system as a public corporation with independent budget and continuous operations. These operations need not be authorized each year by the legislature. As we indicated earlier, the Fund has its own managing board and does not perform under the auspices of any government department as in the case of USAID.

Unlike the regional development banks, the Kuwait Fund obtains its capital through equity transfers from the state budget. Although it is authorized to borrow in the private capital market to the limit of twice its capital and reserves, the Fund has refrained from doing so. Other regional development banks acquire their capital from three resources: 1) paid-in capital; 2) funds raised in capital markets by borrowing on the security of reserves and callable capital; and 3) special funds (Bloch 1968, p. 196). The last two resources constitute a variable determined by the bank's skill in convincing the leaders in the private capital market of its credit-worthiness, as in the case of category (2), or its ability to collect money from outside the region in what amount to political donations that could be made by rich countries for political purposes, as in the case for special funds in category (3). The Kuwait Fund's only source of capital comes from the Kuwaiti govern-

ment in the form of paid-in capital. Responding to a question in a
future-oriented questionnaire, the director general and three other
senior experts thought that the Fund would eventually seek credit in the
private capital market in Kuwait. They could not agree, however, on
the conditions under which the Fund might go into private capital markets as a borrower. There is reason to believe that if the Fund seeks
credit in Kuwait's private markets, it will not be in the near future and
the conditions under which such an action could occur are not clear.
The willingness of the government to supply funds in the form of paid-
in capital would be sufficient for the Fund to meet its possible expansion
in Africa and Asia. If the Fund is to borrow in the private capital market, it will have to change its lending policies and diversify its loans
to include hard loans with interest rates above the present 2 to 4 percent. The pressures on the Kuwait Fund to borrow from private capital
markets could come not only from within the organization, in the case
of expanding operations, but also from private investors in Kuwait.
Those private investors might want to enter the development lending
field if it seems less risky than investing in Western markets, with the
possibility of confiscation or other political dangers. The investment
atmosphere in Western capitalist markets has recently caused doubts
among Arab investors as to how their investments will be treated politically, and how much of their value will be lost through the continuous
erosion of the value of the dollar, pound sterling, and other Western
currencies.

The fact that the Fund does not have to pay interest on capital
enables it to accrue profits from the interest on loans and the returns
on its portfolio investment. Table 3.2 shows the financial statement
for the Fund for two consecutive years, 1972 and 1973. The percentage
of the disbursed funds in relation to total commitments was 72 percent
during 1972-73. The much larger Inter-American Development Bank
had a percentage of disbursements to total commitments of 58 percent
in 1973 (Inter-American Development Bank 1974, p. 15). There were
no available similar data on the African Development Bank, or the
Asian Development Bank. We consider the higher rate of disbursed
funds relative to total commitments as an indicator of higher effectiveness for the Kuwait Fund. The Inter-American Development Bank is
much larger than the Kuwait Fund in terms of geographical scope and
volume of operations, which amounted to $2.8 billion in 1968 and $6.3
billion in 1973 (Inter-American Development Bank 1974). In the case
of IDB, the larger the volume of the operations, the higher was the
rate of disbursements. In 1968, the percentage of the disbursed funds
to total commitment was 48 percent (Singh 1970, p. 31). This means
that IDB became more effective as a vehicle of development aid not
only because of the expansion in its volume of operations, but also because a higher rate of disbursements accompanied that expansion. Two

TABLE 3.2

Balance Sheet of the Kuwait Fund as of March 31, 1973
(in Kuwaiti dinars)

	March 31, 1973	March 31, 1972
Net Assets:		
Cash on hand and in banks	5,491,735	2,792,399
Bank deposits and securities	60,495,701	45,060,960
Loans	102,875,879	99,068,523
Capital participation in the Arab		
Fund	8,400,000	6,000,000
Accrued interest	2,430,681	1,617,287
Sundry debtors	22,833	13,166
Total	179,716,766	149,552,335
Less:		
Loans—undisbursed	28,428,323	27,572,156
Loans—repayment	18,708,688	14,301,215
Sundry credit balance (including		
provisions)	172,937	260,209
Total	47,309,948	107,418,755
Net Worth:		
Statutory capital	200,000,000	200,000,000
Paid-in capital	100,900,000	78,250,000
General reserve	35,506,818	29,168,755
Total	132,406,818	107,418,755

Source: The Kuwait Fund (1973, p. 21).

elements in the effectiveness of a development bank can be distinguished
as separate indicators of effectiveness: the first is the volume of operations (loaned money); the second is the rate of disbursements to total
commitment. The first indicator is a function of the availability of resources; the second is a function of managerial and organizational skill.
IDB was able to more than double its available capital resources between 1968 and 1973. It was able to increase its disbursement rate
from 48 percent to 58 percent. The Kuwait Fund was not as effective
as IDB in increasing its resources during the same period; its total
loan commitments in 1968–69 were KD 68.81 million (The Kuwait Fund
1969, p. 14). The rate of disbursements in the same year was 65.4
percent (The Kuwait Fund 1969, p. 12). If we take the volume of operations and rate of disbursements to total commitments as two indicators
of effectiveness for a development lending agency we find that the Kuwait Fund showed higher effectiveness in its managerial and organiza-

tional skill (measured by the rate of disbursements). The Kuwait Fund
was not as effective in increasing the volume of its operations. The
decision on increasing the volume of operations is linked to the availability of resources, which is determined by the Kuwaiti government's
contribution to the Fund's capital.

An indicator of efficiency for the Kuwait Fund can be shown in
the ratio of administrative expenses (for example, wages, salaries and
remuneration, travel and accommodation and transport expenses, office occupancy [rent] . . . and so on) to total volume of operations. In
the case of the Kuwait Fund the ratio of administrative expenses to
total volume of operations for 1973 was 0.35 percent (The Kuwait Fund
1973, p. 22); the same ratio in 1973 for IDB was 0.66 percent (Inter-
American Development Bank 1974, p. 33). This is another indicator
of managerial and administrative skill in the Kuwait Fund compared
with IDB.

ARAB DEVELOPMENT EXPERTISE IN THE KUWAIT FUND

During March and April 1974 an attitudinal questionnaire was
administered to the professional staff in the Fund.[*] The questionnaire
sought the attitudes of the Fund professionals regarding Arab economic
and political integration; political ideology; and the development process.

The overall rate of response was less than 50 percent. The rate
of response for the senior professionals group, however, was 50 percent (six of the 12 professionals responded to the questionnaire).

This writer noticed that the questions that contained a direct
bearing on the respondent's political views on inter-Arab politics were,
in many cases, left unanswered. We noticed a general reluctance on
the part of the staff members to discuss political issues in a systematic
way as part of the research or to divulge their views on political matters. Some of the objections to questions revealing political attitudes
were made by reference to the "nonpolitical" nature of the Fund and
the need for the staff to remain neutral politically in their dealings with
different Arab regimes. Some of the remarks made in regard to the
political questions in the survey revealed a disdain for politics, which
is not a surprising attitude among professionals in general. An analysis follows of the response to the three broad categories that the questionnaire included.

---

[*]The text of the questionnaire appears in Appendix A.

Arab Identity and Attitude Toward Political
and Economic Unity

A series of questions were designed to identify the intensity of
the respondent attachment to a pan-Arab identity versus insular identities (such as Egyptian, Syrian, Kuwaiti, and so on), and to survey
attitudes and beliefs of the respondent regarding Arab economic and
political integration.

Three questions were intended to establish the pan-Arab identity
of the respondent: the first regarding the Israeli threat to the Arabs
versus the dangers of underdevelopment. The question was phrased,
which of these two problems do you think to be the basic one facing the
Arabs: Israel, or underdevelopment. The second question revolved
around the obligation of rich Arab countries to assist poorer Arab
countries. The third question asked about the respondent's judgment
regarding the contributions of the oil-rich countries to Arab regional
development. The respondent was given three judgments regarding
these contributions: whether they were generous, generous enough, or
less than enough. Since we are interested mainly in assessing the
Fund's role in the context of Kuwait aid, the questionnaire had a question on whether some oil countries contributed more than others to the
cause of Arab development.

In analyzing the responses we will divide them into two groups:
one group represents the senior professional staff, the other the junior
staff members.

The response to the first question regarding whether Israel or
underdevelopment is the basic problem facing the Arabs was as follows:

	Israel	Underdevelopment	Both
Senior staff	1	4	1
Junior staff	—	6	1

It is evident that underdevelopment is perceived to be the basic problem facing the Arabs and not Israel. Only one among the senior professionals and one junior professional thought that both problems were
linked together.

There was almost a consensus among the respondents that rich
Arab countries have an obligation to assist poor Arab countries. Five
of the six senior staff members thought rich Arab countries were obliged to help poor ones while one member was undecided on the issue.
All the junior staff members thought that rich Arabs were obliged to
help poor Arab countries.

When asked whether the contributions of oil countries to Arab
development were generous, generous enough, or less than enough, the
pattern of response differed between the senior staff and the junior staff.

In the senior staff group two members thought the contributions were "enough," two thought they were "less than enough" and two refrained from answering the question.

Among the junior staff members, six thought the contributions were less than enough and only one thought they were enough.

There was unanimous agreement among the respondents that Kuwait, among Arab oil countries, made more contributions than others toward Arab development. Two respondents mentioned Abu-Dhabi with Kuwait as among those oil countries that contributed more to Arab development.

The conclusions from these responses can be drawn as follows:

• The pan-Arab identity among the professionals is rather strong. This can be shown in the unanimous agreement that rich Arab countries are obliged to assist poor Arab countries.

• The pan-Arab identity is more strongly expressed among members of the junior staff than the senior staff. This is shown in the judgment of the oil countries' contribution to Arab development. The junior staff almost unanimously thought the contributions were less than enough. The senior staff were more ambivalent in taking a position; two refrained from answering the question; two thought the contributions were enough. It should be noted that the question is more sensitive for a senior non-Kuwaiti staff member to answer than it is for a junior Kuwaiti staff member. The writer noticed a general reluctance on the part of the senior staff members to express strong personal views regarding sensitive issues that involve inter-Arab politics or the policies of the Kuwait government. The whole survey should be perceived in this context, and the results of the survey are interpreted with this caveat in mind.

• We believe that the staff responses (both senior and junior) to the question on the Israeli problem reflected the influence of profession and career on views and attitudes. The question was designed as an indicator of the pan-Arab identity of the respondent. It was assumed that if respondents chose Israel as the basic problem facing the Arab countries, they would rank higher on a scale of Arab nationalism than if they chose underdevelopment as the basic problem. There was almost unanimous agreement among the respondents that underdevelopment was the basic problem facing the Arab countries. This response has to be explained in view of the influence of a person's career on his judgment. These professionals are engaged in a lifetime career the objective of which is to get rid of underdevelopment in the Arab countries or at least to mitigate the negative effects of underdevelopment. They are more familiar with the problems associated with underdevelopment than they are with any other public problem. This explains their choice of underdevelopment as the basic problem facing the Arab countries. Only one among the senior professionals thought that Israel was the basic problem facing the Arabs.

With the caveats mentioned earlier we conclude that the Arab identity of the professionals of the Fund is strong—stronger, however, among the junior staff than among the senior staff. The professional orientation is very evident among the respondents and it leads them to be less politically oriented. As mentioned before, there was a sense of disdain of politics among the staff, and their apolitical orientation is particularly reflected in their perceptions regarding the basic problem facing the Arabs.

The respondents' views on Arab economic and political integration show a moderate degree of optimism and tend to confirm our conclusion regarding the presence of a noticeable pan-Arab identity among the staff. When asked whether they were "satisfied with the present level of economic cooperation among Arab countries," all the senior staff members responded negatively. Only two of the junior staff members said that they were moderately satisfied with the present level of inter-Arab economic cooperation, while the rest were dissatisfied.

The respondents were asked to give their beliefs regarding economic integration in the Arab world. Three statements were given in which economic integration ranged from "a far reaching goal that requires many changes in the structure of Arab countries," to "a possibility that could be worked out if the Arabs are interested enough," to "an urgent necessity for the sake of a more rapid development in the Arab World." More of the senior professionals believed Arab economic integration to be a possibility (50 percent of them). Two of the senior staff members believed it was an urgent necessity, while one believed it to be a far-reaching goal. The junior staff members were firmer believers in the necessity for Arab economic integration. Four of the seven respondents believed Arab economic integration to be "an urgent necessity," two believed it "a possibility," while one believed it a far-reaching goal.

The staff was asked about the feasibility of economic unity and political unity and the likelihood of achieving one without the other. The question was phrased with certain assumptions in mind about the integration process. Long-time students of regional integration indicate that the integration process is complimentary in nature, that integration can proceed in certain spheres of social life up to a point where the momentum is lost if it is not reinforced by a similar integrative process in other fields. The spillover concept is always assumed to be an important concept in integration studies. Another important aspect is the decision-making center in any integration process; the processes of interest conflict and conciliation, elite socialization and social learning are mentioned as elements that work in the integrative process to blur sectoral lines in such a process. It is generally assumed that the political domain is an essential ingredient in an integrative process (Hass 1970), (Caporaso 1971).

Three statements were made for the respondent to choose from about economic unity and political unity: economic unity is easier to achieve than political unity; political unity is easier to achieve than economic unity; economic unity and political unity in the Arab world are inseparable and achieving one would entail the other.

From what we know about the integration process (which is very little as admitted by long-time students of the subject), any economic integration involves a political decision. Moreover, in a situation such as that existing in the Arab world, economic unity seems a dependent variable that changes according to the political wills that exist in the various Arab countries. The results of the October 1973 War confirm such a conceptualization. When the Arabs found more common ground for political agreements, many concerted initiatives emerged on the economic cooperation level. The movement toward using oil as a political weapon enhanced the chances of economic cooperation among the Arab countries and facilitated the inter-Arab movement of economic resources. It is recognized in Kuwait and elsewhere in the Arab world that the spur in economic cooperation that happened after October 1973 was a result of a temporary agreement on common political objectives.

The response of the Fund professionals to the statements made regarding economic and political unity in the Arab world reflects an insular view of Arab economic integration. Five senior staff members thought economic unity easier to achieve than political unity and ignored the possibility that both are inseparable in the case of the Arab world. In the junior professional group, such a realization of the inseparability of economic unity and political unity was more evident. Three thought economic unity and political unity were inseparable while four thought that economic unity was easier to achieve than political unity.

The senior professionals tended to perceive economic unity in a different perspective than political unity and to dismiss a strong relationship between the two; their response to statements about Arab unity showed that they were not strong believers in the possibility of an Arab nation-state. While they dismiss the notion that Arab unity is a "romantic dream of the past," they also believe that it is not "a definite policy goal that can be realized in the near future." The statement about Arab unity which was accepted by the majority of the senior staff (four of the six) read "Arab unity is a distant goal in the future that could be achieved if the various Arab countries planned carefully to reduce differences in political, economic and social conditions prevailing in various Arab countries." The other two members believed that "Arab unity is a definite policy goal that can be realized in the near future if Arab leaders are sincere about it."

In the junior professionals group, beliefs about Arab unity were similar to those of the senior professional group. Six of the seven respondents viewed Arab unity as a "distant goal in the future," and only one believed it to be a "definite policy goal."

Political Ideology

This part of the attitudinal survey aimed at viewing the respondents on a political continuum that has liberal, Western-oriented attitudes at one pole and a radical socialist (a form of Marxism either Soviet or Chinese) at the other pole. Political views were sought regarding certain issues where the distinction could be made between a radical-socialist and a liberal-democrat. In order to accommodate possible variations of political opinion regarding certain issues, more choices were given that refer to such possible attitudes as human socialism and Islamic fundamentalism. In a question regarding the reasons for the 1967 defeat of the Arabs in their third war against Israel and the possible strategies to achieve victory, three main political trends were presented and the respondent was asked to make a choice. The question was based on a survey of intellectual and political trends that were in discussion in Arab intellectual and political circles after the 1967 defeat (Dessouki 1973). The question was phrased as follows:

After 1967 there have been many political and intellectual dialogues in the Arab world about the reasons for the defeat and the road to victory. I will give you a sample of three trends to choose the one you find most agreeable to you.
    a) a secular-liberal trend represented by Dr. Constantine Zuraik who sees the reasons for the defeat in Arab cultural and technological backwardness. The road to victory is to become more modern in the Western sense: to absorb Western technology and social values, to industrialize, to separate state from religion . . . etc.
    b) an Islamic religious trend represented by Dr. Salah Eddin El-Munajjid who sees the reasons for the defeat in the decay of religion and decline of Islam in the Arab world. Going back to the basic and true teachings of Islam would give the Arabs a new sense of courage and dignity which would be the road to victory.
    c) a revolutionary socialist trend represented by Dr. Sadek Jalal Al-Azm who sees the defeat as a natural outcome of the decay of traditional bourgeois Arab regimes.

The road to victory would be a revolution of scientific
socialism that does away with all the existing methods
of social organization and production and brings about
a new way of life based on a new ideology of man and
science.

The response of the staff to the question showed its reluctance
to accept either one of the categories by itself as representative of its
views. The stereotypes of trends represented in the question did not
perfectly appeal to the respondents, especially the senior staff. Only
two of the senior staff members chose (a), and one chose (b). None of
the senior staff members accepted the Marxist revolutionary trend represented in (c). Two of the respondents among the senior professionals
chose a modified combination of (a) and (b) (that is, the acceptance of
Western techniques but in a fit that is appropriate for the Arab culture
in which Islam is a prominent element). One such respondent mentioned
the need to "absorb Western technology while indigenous social values
should be developed in the context of Arab culture." One senior staff
member did not accept any of the three opinions presented in the question concerning the reasons for 1967 defeat and the road to victory.
Rather, he indicated the reason for the defeat to be "loss of confidence
in ourselves and in our cultural identity." He also indicated that what
the Arabs need now is soul-searching for a new ideology that reflects
the true cultural values of the Arabs in which the spiritual element is
more important than the material one.

The junior staff response was more straightforward than that of
the senior staff. Two chose (a) and two chose (b) while three of them
abstained from answering.

It is significant that none of the respondents in either group accepted the Marxist revolutionary trend. Those who abstained from
answering among the junior professionals did not do so because they
were unwilling to show their Marxist leanings. They abstained from
answering for reasons other than being Marxist without the desire to
explicate their ideology.

On the validity of Western democracy as a political system that
is appropriate for the Arabs, the answer diverged markedly between
the junior staff and the senior staff as shown below:

Respondent	Yes	No	Undecided
Senior staff	2	1	3
Junior staff	4	2	1

The senior staff members were more skeptical on whether
Western democracy is the best political system for the Arabs, while
the junior staff members were more positive in choosing Western democracy as the best political system. It should be noted that most of

the junior staff members are Kuwaitis. The political system of Kuwait has the formal appearance of a parliamentary democratic system because the National Assembly is elected and it serves as a legislative organ for the state. Laws have to be approved by the Assembly before they are enacted. Although the executive branch is always headed by the Crown Prince, and the head of state (the Amir) has ultimate power regarding both the executive and the legislative branches of government (that is, he can dissolve the parliament and remove the government), many Kuwaitis perceive their political system to be a parliamentary democracy on the Western model.

In a question about the adequacy of different social systems to meet human needs, the response among the senior group showed difference of opinion, while the majority of the junior group chose a capitalist welfare system. The question gave four choices that presumably reflect different socio-political systems with different values. The question read: "The majority of the people (that is, the masses) have the best human conditions in: Yugoslavia ___, the Soviet Union ___, the United States ___, or China ___."

Three of the senior professionals refrained from answering, while two of them chose the United States and one chose China. The junior group was clearly more in favor of the United States (four out of seven), while two abstained from answering and one chose China.

Another question tended to confirm the beliefs of the respondents toward social systems by focusing on the existing systems in the Arab world. The question read: "What is the Arab country that comes closer than any other Arab country in taking care of the interest of its masses?" There was an overwhelming response among the junior group: all of the seven respondents thought the answer to be Kuwait. The senior group's response was consistent with their answer to the previously mentioned question about the social systems. In their response, one chose Kuwait, another chose Algeria, while three abstained from answering and one mentioned that no Arab country comes close to taking care of the interests of its masses.

A third question tried to round the view of the staff preferences concerning different social systems in the context of the Arab world. The question read: "If you were given your present income doing a similar job, what Arab country (other than Kuwait) would you choose to live in and work for the rest of your life?" Those who chose their home country were asked to make another preference in order to remove family reasons from affecting the choice. The answer is shown in the following:

Respondents	Lebanon	Egypt	Morocco	Tunisia	Bahrain	No Answer
Senior staff	2	1	—	1	—	2
Junior staff	2	2	1	—	1	1

The assumption behind the question is that different Arab countries have different stereotypes that reflect different values. For example, Lebanon has the stereotype of a Westernized liberal democracy with a parliamentary system of government, free press, and capitalist economic system. Egypt has the stereotype of a socialist country with a controlled economy, and less access to the variety and quality of consumer goods that a capitalist economy like that of Lebanon offers. Egypt has a more Arab flavor to its social life than does Lebanon. Tunisia and Morocco have a distinct image of being heavily influenced by their French colonial heritage (in the intellectual circles of Rabat and Tunis, French is more prevalently spoken than Arabic). Their image includes also a more liberal economy with availability of Western consumer goods. Syria and Iraq offer an image of a more socialist character and a more politically and economically controlled social life than the rest of the Arab countries. Aside from the abstention of two senior staff members and one junior staff member from answering the question, we found more of the senior staff members opting for Lebanon (2), than for Egypt (1), with another choosing Tunisia (which for our purposes comes close to choosing Lebanon in terms of indicating a preference for a certain social system). The junior staff members were equally divided in their choice of Lebanon and Egypt (two each), with one preference for Morocco and one for Bahrain. Bahrain is a traditional society with a tribal structure of social and political life.

In concluding about the political ideology of the Fund professionals we note the following:

It is very difficult to categorize the senior staff members in a specific political grouping. Their response to the various questions reflected a multiplicity of views and preferences that could not be readily categorized under an easy all-encompassing label. With this general comment, we can say that the liberal democratic attitude can be found more or less explicit among a minority of the senior staff members. Two of them chose the liberal secular attitude toward the causes of the 1967 defeat and possible remedies to its negative effects. Two chose Western democratic systems as the "best" political system for the Arabs. Two thought the majority of people had the best human conditions in the United States. Two chose Lebanon as the place to work and live for the rest of their lives, and one chose a social setting similar to that of Lebanon (Tunisia). It is fair to say that if any one political attitude is explicitly presented among the senior staff members, it is the Western liberal democratic attitude. No other categorical political attitude is articulated in their response. A socio-political Marxist attitude is almost nonexistent. Islamic fundamentalism, as a political trend expressed in the aftermath of the 1967 war intellectual dialogue in the Arab world, was able to secure one choice among the senior staff members' responses. As a trend, however, Islamic fundamentalism was not confirmed by the response to other questions.

From the comments made regarding the question on the 1967 war
and on Western democracy as being the best political system, we can
say that the majority of the senior staff members in the Fund realize
the need for achieving a synthesis between modern technological and
material achievements, and Arab cultural and social values. It is obvious to anyone working in the field of economic and social development
that modern technology, (which is increasingly becoming part of a uni-
versal culture) is essential to any effort in raising the standard of living
of a certain people and overcoming poverty, malnutrition, poor health
and illiteracy. From the experiences of post-World War II development
in the Soviet Union, Eastern Europe, China, and Japan, the role of
modern technology is seen as an essential part in any developmental
process. It is realized that technological advances in the fields of industry, agriculture, communication, health, and education that were
made during the past 50 years in the West, have now become an essential part of any development process in any part of the world. This
technological aspect of the development process, however, need not
take the same form in every society. A process of adaptation is essential to the success of technological transfers. This is what happened
in the case of the socialist countries in Eastern Europe and China, and
also in the case of a version of capitalist social organization in Japan.
What the majority of the senior staff members of the Fund believe in
is a political ideology that represents a synthesis of modern technological base with Arab cultural values. Certain basic elements in Western
democracies appeal to the Arabs such as the concept of representation,
and freedom of expression, but an integrated picture of a Western democratic system is not seen as the best political system that the Arabs
can have. Three of the respondents were undecided concerning the
relevance of Western democratic systems to the Arabs. They could
neither respond negatively nor positively because they had a selective
orientation toward the concept. Some of the elements of a liberal democratic system are accepted and some are rejected.

The junior group had a more evident preference for a Western
liberal democratic capitalist system. Four of the seven respondents
thought that Western democracy was the best political system for the
Arabs. Four believed that the majority of the people had the best human
conditions in the United States. All of the respondents thought that Kuwait was the Arab country that came closer than any other Arab country
in taking care of the interests of its masses.

Although these responses show that a majority of the junior staff
members had attitudes indicating a preference for a Western liberal
democratic political system with a capitalist economy, this attitude
was by no means unanimous. In their response to the question on the
1967 Arab defeat, two chose the liberal-secular attitude and two chose
the Islamic fundamentalist attitude, while three abstained. In their

choice for a country to live and work in for the rest of their lives, other than Kuwait, two chose Lebanon, two chose Egypt, one chose Morocco, one chose Bahrain, and one abstained.

The choices made regarding these two questions indicate that the general trend toward a democratic liberal political attitude and a preference for a capitalist system is modified by an Islamic religious trend and the existence of preferences in social systems other than those of a capitalist character. The choices for Bahrain and Egypt, although they indicated value preferences for a socially controlled economy (Egypt) and a traditional mode of social organization (Bahrain), certainly did not represent an element of political radicalism. The general attitudes of the junior professionals were moderately liberal with a certain appreciation for Arab cultural and social organization.

Perceptions of the Development Process

Part of the attitudinal survey aimed at forming an image of how the Fund professionals perceive the development process. The questions tried to get at the views of the respondents regarding such issues as the value of efficiency as the main criterion for governmental action in the field of development, the value of financing productive activities versus social-type projects, the importance of different actors in the development process such as politicians, planners, and administrators, and the relevance of the contributions made by various social scientists toward understanding the development process.

Few of the responses of the junior and senior staff groups showed common perceptions regarding development.

In a question about the nature of the concept of "national development" there was unanimous agreement among the senior staff members that development is a concept that has economic, political, and sociological components. Only one of the junior staff members perceived "national development" to be an economic concept while the rest of them agreed with the senior group that it is a multi-faceted concept. Another issue that reflected common views was the concept of efficiency. A statement on efficiency was presented with the possibility of agreeing, disagreeing, or being undecided about the statement. The statement read: "Efficiency should be the prime goal of any government interested in promoting development." Five of the senior staff members agreed with the statement while one disagreed. Six of the junior staff members agreed with the statement while one disagreed.

Other than agreeing on these two general issues: the concept of national development and the importance of efficiency, the senior staff and the junior staff groups showed different perceptions regarding the various issues related to development.

Two questions were asked about the relative importance of the different actors as related to the outcome of the development process and the relative importance of the different activities constituting a developmental action. The first question read:

If you are asked to generalize from your experience and knowledge of Arab countries, what they need most to improve their conditions is: (Please choose one)
a) good and devoted political leaders who give high priority to development and make necessary sacrifices.
b) good planners and economists who would set up economically sound plans that will help the country achieve development.
c) good managers and administrators who would turn even modest plans into success.

The answer to the question is shown in the following:

Respondents	Political leaders	Planners and Economists	Managers and Administrators
Senior group	3	—	3
Junior group	1	2	4

The second question asked the respondent to order hierarchically by relative importance the different elements in achieving national development: "Success of national development depends on the following conditions: (please arrange in order of importance) a) good political system; b) good planning models and well thought through plans; c) good administrative system; d) other important factors."

The response to the question is shown in Table 3.3. These two questions were intended to assess the degree to which there is an "economistic" orientation among the staff members toward development. There was an assumption that the staff tended to perceive the development process in economic terms and to emphasize the role of economists and economic measurements of the development process. This assumption was based partially on the emphasis the Fund attached to its professional image as a development lending institution. The response to those two questions does not support the assumption. In fact the response reflected a more rounded image of the development process among the members of the senior staff than it was assumed. None of the senior staff thought that what the Arab countries needed most in order to achieve successful development was good planners and economists. Half of them thought that what were needed most were good and devoted political leaders; the other half thought that good managers and administrators were what were needed most. Their response to the second question tended to confirm this view of development. The

TABLE 3.3

The Relative Importance of Different Elements
in Achieving National Development

| | Respondents | |
	Senior Group	Junior Group
Political system		
First	1	2
Second	1	—
Third	2	4
Planning models		
First	—	3
Second	1	2
Third	1	1
Administrative system		
First	3	2
Second	2	4
Third	—	1
Ideology		
First	2	—
Second	—	—
Third	—	—
Resources and technology		
First	—	—
Second	—	—
Third	1	—

first most important element in achieving development was not good
plans; three believed it to be good administrative system; two thought
it sound developmental ideology; one thought it good political system.
Among their ranking of the three most important elements in achieving
development, a good administrative system was chosen five times; a
good political system was chosen four times; while good plans were
chosen twice, once as a second most important element and once as
the third most important element.

The response of the junior staff reflected a slight tendency toward
an economistic view of development. This tendency was by no means
very strong among the junior staff members as a group. Only two of
the seven respondents thought that good planners and economists were
what the Arab countries needed most to achieve successful development.
Four opted for good managers and administrators while one opted for
good political leaders. In their ranking of the priorities of different

elements in achieving development, good planning models were mentioned three times to be the first most important element, two times as the second most important element and once as the third most important element. In its ranking among the three most important elements in achieving development, a good administrative system was mentioned more often than good planning models. The political system was thought to be less important than the administrative system and planning models in achieving development. The overall ranking of the importance of the various elements in achieving development shows the administrative system to be the most important one in the total rankings made by both the junior staff and the senior staff. This view of the special importance of the administrative factor in achieving development has also been reiterated in the statements of the director general of the Fund.

Another question was included in the survey which sought the staff opinion regarding the value of professional contributions to development made by the various technical expertise and the disciplines of social sciences. Three consecutive questions asked the respondent how he perceived the value of the contributions of political scientists, experts on administration, and sociologists to the work of planning boards in the Arab countries. The respondent was asked to evaluate the contributions of each type of expertise in terms of whether it would lead to better performance, worse performance, or would not make any difference in the quality of work of the planning boards in the Arab countries. The response was as follows:

Respondents	Political Experts			Administration Experts			Sociology Experts		
	Better	Worse	No Change	Better	Worse	No Change	Better	Worse	No Change
Senior staff	2	2	2	6	—	—	6	—	—
Junior staff	—	6	1	5	—	—	5	—	—

The response to the question shows the beliefs of the staff, both senior and junior, held in regard to the importance of the administrative aspects of development. It also shows that they believe that experts on administration can improve the work of the planning boards. While both senior and junior staff believed in the importance of a good political system and devoted political leaders to a better development performance, they showed disbelief in regard to the ability of political scientists to improve the product of planning boards in the Arab countries. This should not be surprising, especially to political scientists (Ilchman and Uphoff 1969, p. vii). The response shows that the assumption about an economistic orientation of the staff regarding development does not hold. There was almost unanimous agreement that sociologists can contribute positively to a better performance of the planning boards.

As shown earlier, the Fund lending pattern indicates that it shuns financing social projects such as education, health, and family planning. A series of three questions tried to seek the staff professional views towards financing social projects. The three questions read as follows:

(a) In the Arab countries generally, social projects such as education and health are difficult to finance because of lack of interest on the part of funding institutions:
agree _____   disagree _____   undecided _____
(b) It is difficult, in the present development of cost/benefit analysis to measure satisfactorily and with precision the benefits of such social projects as education, health care, and family planning:
agree _____   disagree _____   undecided _____
(c) The difficulty in measuring the benefits of a social project is:
_____ a major reason for the difficulty to get it financed
_____ a minor reason for the difficulty to get it financed
_____ has no connection to get it financed

The response to (a) was as follows:

Respondent	Agree	Disagree	Undecided	No Answer
Senior staff	3	1	1	1
Junior staff	3	3	1	1

The response to (b) was as follows:

Respondent	Agree	Disagree	Undecided	No Answer
Senior staff	3	2	—	1
Junior staff	5	1	—	1

The response to (c) was as follows:

Respondent	Major Reason	Minor Reason	No Connection	No Answer
Senior staff	—	1	5	—
Junior staff	4	1	—	2

The three questions were aimed at arriving at an answer regarding the reluctance of the Fund and other similar institutions to finance social projects. There might be two explanations why the Fund does not finance social projects: 1) technical reasons (difficulties in evaluating satisfactorily the benefits of social projects and consequently reluctance to underwrite costs); 2) policy reasons.

From the response of the senior staff we see that technical reasons, in their view, cannot be the main reason why the Kuwait Fund shuns financing social projects. Five of the six senior staff members who responded to the questionnaire thought that the difficulty in measuring the benefits of social projects had no connection with the ability to get financing for such projects. One senior staff member thought that it was a minor reason.

A final point in the survey involved learning how the economists among the members of the staff perceived the discipline of economics and the contributions of the more frequently mentioned Western economists to our understanding of the development process.

A question asked for an evaluation of the progress of economics as a discipline in the last two decades, whether progress could be attributed to the development of econometrics (more mathematical orientation of the discipline), or to improved communications and understanding with other fields of social science such as politics, sociology, anthropology, and organization theory.

The senior staff thought that progress in economics resulted from its being more mathematically oriented (three responses) rather than from improving communications with other social science disciplines (one response). The junior staff thought that progress in economics was due to improved communications with other social sciences (four responses), rather than its being more mathematically oriented (two responses).

When asked which economists they thought made lasting contributions to development studies, the staff (both senior and junior) made reference to such names as Chenery, Nurkse, Tinbergen, Harrod and Domar, Kuznets, A. Lewis, Myrdal, and Rostow. The list included the more conventional contributors to development economics except for Myrdal and Rostow. When asked to mention three printed works that they thought were very important for someone who works in the field of development to have read, the list included the more conventional works of the previously mentioned authors. This writer expected Hirschman to be mentioned with his rather important work on "Development Projects Observed," valuable for anyone who works in the field of development lending.

The overall results of this survey showed the Kuwait Fund staff to have an evident pan-Arab identification, to be more on the liberal side in terms of their political ideology, but with a definite attachment to Arab cultural values. They are eclectic in their approach to Western democracy and Western material and social values. The question of identification with parochial country identities (such as Egypt, Syria or Sudan), versus a more pan-Arab identification cannot be totally answered by results of this attitudinal survey. It is important, however, to mention a recent debate in an Egyptian specialized political

quarterly about the issue of Egyptian nationalism versus Arab nationalism. In a recent article (Ghali 1974), an Egyptian writer tried to
argue for the existence of an Egyptian identity based on a certain concept of Egyptian nationalism. The writer could not define the elements
of Egyptian nationalism, although he argued for its existence. He con-
tended that it Egyptian nationality had been defined several decades
ago, the instability and perplexity in policies and the extreme shifts
in direction that characterized the Nasser era in Egypt would have been
avoided (Ghali 1974, pp. 278-83). Ghali stated that "there is an Egyptian cultural heritage of which the Arab culture is an important part,
and there is an Egyptian nationalism of which Arabism is one important element" (Ghali 1974, p. 297). This sample of intellectual attitudes
toward Arab nationalism has been widely discussed recently in the
printed media in Egypt. To gauge how much influence this attitude has
among Egyptian intellectuals is not part of this study. What we are
interested in is to show that such an attitude is not existent among the
Fund's Arab staff, including the Egyptians. It is also significant to
note that in the following issue of International Politics where the article by Ghali appeared, some Egyptian intellectuals (including university professors, writers, and social scientists engaged in research),
took the Ghali article to task, questioning its historical and scientific
validity and methodological rigor.

THE KUWAIT FUND AND ARAB SURPLUS CAPITAL

It is obvious that the increase in oil prices that OPEC instituted
after the October 1973 War has had far-reaching implications not only
in terms of accumulating more wealth for the Arab oil-producing countries, but also in terms of the possible role that such wealth could play
in an Arab regional context and in the international financial system.
We are concerned here with the possible role that the Arab surplus can
play in developing the Arab countries. It is in this context that the Kuwait Fund comes to play an important role in influencing the use of
Arab surplus funds for internal development of the Arab region.
Many estimates were made about the volume of Arab surplus
capital that is expected to be floating in the international financial system in the next decade, (Akins 1973), (Al-Hamad 1973a), (Mabro and
Monroe 1974), (Rustow 1974), (Shihata 1974b). We are interested in
the estimates that are made by the Arabs themselves in a more or less
official forum. The Arab Fund for Economic and Social Development
conducted a study on the flow of financial resources in the Arab world
which assumed that, if production of oil is held constant on the December 1972 levels (which is a little less than the October 6, 1973 level

and more than the November 1973 level) and prices of oil are that of the December 1973 level, the surplus funds available for the Arab oil producing countries will amount to \$210-260 billion by the end of 1985 (Shihata 1974b, p. 5).

The Arab surplus is affecting the Kuwait Fund in more than one way. It goes without saying that the Kuwait government's decision to increase the Fund's capital from KD 200 million to KD 1 billion was made possible and was partly motivated by the increase in government revenue resulting from the increase in oil prices. At the same time the accumulation of an Arab surplus poses a challenge to the Kuwait Fund and other Arab financial institutions: how to use the accumulated surplus in promoting Arab development. It is evident to any Arab financial manager that Western currencies are becoming a less and less effective means for the storage of value for the accumulated Arab funds. The erosion in the value of the once respected Western currencies is posing a serious problem to holders of large quantities of such currencies. During 1971-73, the Kuwait Fund lost \$13.3 million because of the devaluation of the dollar (Al-Hamad 1973b, p. 15), and the total dollar holdings of the Fund during those two years would be negligible compared with the dollar holdings of Arab governments in the next decade.

The Arab surplus funds have at least four outlets: to be used for the development of internal economies in the oil-producing countries; to be used for financing inter-Arab development projects in the Arab world; to be used for investing in world oil industry (in exploration, refining, and transportation of oil); and to be used for investments in equities in the international capital market or for purchase of real estate in the industrialized West. The use of Arab surplus in promoting Arab regional development is one alternative that has to compete for Arab funds with the other three alternatives. From a political and economic point of view, the most vocal competitor for the use of Arab surplus will be the development of the internal economies of the oil-producing countries. There is a definite limit, however, on the amount of surplus that can be absorbed by these economies internally, especially in the coming few years. We already mentioned the risks involved in the international capital market for political and economic reasons. Investment in the international oil industry is a reasonable outlet for the Arab surplus in which all Arab oil-producing countries can cooperate. The only limitations such an outlet presents will be conflict of interest between Arab countries and giant oil companies. Also, the shortage in managerial and technical know-how on the part of the Arab oil-producing countries limits the chances of those countries to invest heavily in the international oil industry.

The investment in Arab regional development can be a major outlet for the Arab surplus, but still it is surrounded with problems.

Economic problems of raising the absorptive capacity of Arab economies represent one kind of such problems (El-Mallakh 1974).

Another kind of problem is of a political nature. Risks of confiscation, expropriation, and restrictions on the transfer of returns on investments to countries of origin are all still obstacles that stand in the way of greater investments by Arab oil countries in capital-deficit Arab countries. In the present context, it is safe to assume that drastic increases in the flow of capital from Arab oil countries to the rest of Arab countries is unlikely "unless significant political changes take place" (Mabro and Monroe 1974, p. 22). What we mean by drastic increases is that inter-Arab investment becomes the major outlet for Arab surplus. It is reasonable to assume that closer political cooperation among the Arab countries is as important a step in that direction as are technical and economic measures to increase the absorptive capacities of the nonoil-producing Arab countries. Profitable investments could be made in Egyptian industry, in irrigation projects in Syria, in agriculture and transport in Sudan, and in light industries and services in Lebanon (Mabro and Monroe 1974, p. 22).

The Kuwait Fund has acknowledged its task in making the Arab surplus a more effective contributor to Arab development. The director of the Fund acknowledged that the Arab financial strategists should have two considerations in mind: that of keeping the value of their surplus from deteriorating, and using as much of that surplus as possible in promoting regional Arab development.

> The strategy that Arab surplus funds should follow must,
> in my opinion, take into consideration both these aspects
> of the situation and try to maximize the advantages to be
> reaped in international financial markets while endeavor-
> ing simultaneously to increase the absorptive capacity of
> Arab economies and promote the flow of investment into
> their most development-oriented sectors (Al-Hamad
> 1973b, p. 8).

Al-Hamad proposed a strategy for improving the absorptive capacity of the Arab economies through collaboration of Arab capital with "['multinational corporations'] entrepreneurial and managerial capabilities, technical know-how, marketing and demand opportunities, and even the availability of material and financial resources." (Al-Hamad 1973b, p. 11). During the early months of 1975 there were reports in Kuwaiti newspapers suggesting a plan to invest the major part of the surplus accruing to Arab oil exporting countries in the Arab world. Kuwait seemed to be particularly interested in promoting regional Arab economic cooperation and development. If the linking ties between Kuwait and the rest of the Arab region are economically strong, then when oil is completely depleted from the oil field, Kuwait can still share in an overall more developed Arab region which she was instrumental in creating. The Kuwait Fund seems to be the natural arm of the Kuwait government in promoting concepts and policies related to the encouragement of the use of Arab surplus funds inside the Arab region. Kuwaitis are aware that if they "fail to adopt adequate development policies" internally and on the Arab regional level, they may end up "in a situation worse, from the social as well as the human point of view, than before the oil era" (Al-Hamad 1973a, p. 4).

4

INSTITUTIONS OF
REGIONAL DEVELOPMENT
IN THE ARAB WORLD:
A POLICY APPRAISAL

This chapter deals with another institution that has a similar objective to that of the Kuwait Fund, the Arab Fund for Economic and Social Development. We are interested, in the present chapter, in perceiving the relative advantages and disadvantages of national institutions performing regional functions (such as the Kuwait Fund) and multinational institutions performing regional functions (such as the Arab Fund).

We argued before that national institutions have their paramount goal in serving the interests of an individual state. In the case of the Kuwait Fund, its regional functions assume their importance because Kuwait's government perceives such regional functions to be of political significance in the context of inter-Arab politics. Earlier, we pointed to the possible contradiction which might arise because of the special nature of a national institution performing regional functions. *

In this chapter we shall deal with the Arab Fund for Economic and Social Development as a multinational institution performing regional development functions. We shall deal with the structure of the Arab Fund, its organizational dynamics, and operational policies. We shall try to point to relative strengths and weaknesses of the Kuwait Fund and the Arab Fund as two different institutional instruments working in the field of Arab regional development. Special attention will be paid to a preliminary appraisal of the Arab Fund as an instrument of Arab regional development and cooperation.

---

*See Chapter 3, pp. 52-53

THE ARAB FUND: ORGANIZATIONAL STRUCTURE AND DYNAMICS

We indicated earlier that the finally adopted agreement establishing the Arab Fund resembled in many ways the World Bank's Articles of Agreement. In terms of the adopted organizational arrangements governing the Arab Fund, the framework resembles that of the World Bank. In this section we shall deal first with the management of the Arab Fund as a multinational organization, its internal organization, and finally, with the organizational doctrine and dynamics of the Arab Fund.

The Management of the Arab Fund

The Arab Fund came into creation when 12 Arab countries signed the establishing agreement on May 16, 1968. The countries which were the founding members of the Arab Fund include Jordan, Tunisia, Algeria, Sudan, Iraq, Syria, Libya, Egypt, North and South Yemen, Kuwait, Lebanon, Morocco, United Arab Emirates, Bahrain, and Qatar.

The authorized capital of the Arab Fund is 100 million Kuwaiti dinars of which KD 81 million is subscribed by the founding members, firstly, in two initial installments, each amounting to 10 percent of the value of shares allotted to them, to be paid up on ratification and the Agreement's entering into force; and then subsequently 10 equal annual installments (articles 5 and 7 of the Agreement).

The shares allotted to the founding members are as follows:[*]

	KD Thousands
Jordan	2,500
Tunisia	500
Algeria	4,000
Sudan	1,500
Iraq	7,500
Syria	3,000
Libya	12,000
Egypt	10,500
Yemen Arab Republic (North Yemen)	500
Kuwait	30,000
Lebanon	1,000
Morocco	2,000

---

[*]For recent additions to the Arab Fund membership and the increase in its capital, see Appendix C.

Yemen Democratic Republic (South Yemen)	10
United Arab Emirates	5,000
Bahrain	500
Qatar	1,000

The Arab Fund as a multinational development organization makes its policy decisions according to a voting system that reflects the financial contribution of the member states. The Arab Fund is managed, or more properly, controlled by a board of governors, each governor representing his country and casting a vote reflecting the relative financial contribution of that country. The voting structure, however, has an equalizing element effecting the influence of the various member countries by allotting a flat rate of 200 votes to each member. Then according to the sum that a country subscribes in the total capital, it is given one vote for each share of KD 10,000. The voting power of the members ranges from as small as 201 (South Yemen) to as large as 3,200 (Kuwait).

The Arab Fund is managed through two layers of decision-making units: the board of governors, which is the highest policy and decision unit, and the board of directors, which executes the policies formulated by the board of governors. The president of the Arab Fund is the chairman of the board of directors and he offers the link between the two tiers of decision units. He is also the head of the employees in the Arab Fund, represents the Fund in its dealings with the member governments and other national and international institutions.

The Board of Governors

Each member state appoints a governor and an alternate governor for a five-year period to represent the state in the board of governors' annual meetings. The period for which a governor or an alternate is appointed is renewable. Each member state can, however, change its governor or alternate at any time.

The board of governors holds annual meetings and a chairman is elected annually to chair the board's meeting. The board of governors can be convened upon the request of at least three of the members who muster 25 percent of the total number of votes, or upon the request of the board of directors. The quorum for the meetings of the board of governors is attained when a majority of the members representing two-thirds of the total votes are present.

The board of governors is the highest policy decision center, although it might not be the formulator of policy. Due to the nature of the Arab Fund as a multinational organization, there are specific functions that can be undertaken only by the board of governors while the rest are delegated to the president or the board of directors. These exclusive functions include acceptance of new members into the Arab Fund, authorization of increases in the capital of the Arab Fund, suspension of a member state, resolution of disputes related to the interpretation of the Articles of Agreement, conclusion of treaties with other international institutions aimed at increasing the cooperation with such institutions, and the dissolution of the Arab Fund and termination of its operations and specification as to how the Arab Fund's net income be dispensed with.

In the first meeting of the board of governors in Kuwait City in February 1972, the board elected the governor of Kuwait to be chairman of the board of governors for the following year. During the second meeting in Kuwait in 1973, the governor of Lebanon was elected chairman of the board and it was decided to hold the third meeting of the board in Beirut in April 1974. In these board meetings policy guidelines are voiced by the various governors. Of special importance is the policy statement given by the chairman of the board.

The Board of Directors

The board of directors conducts the management of the Fund's activities within the guidelines set by the board of governors. The board of directors consists of four full-time "Arab citizens" known for "expertise and efficiency" who are elected by the board of governors for two years, term renewable. Each of the four directors has an alternate. The four directors and their alternates are elected by the board of governors. Each governor nominates a person to be director and another for alternate. The four directors and their alternates are elected in a majority vote by the board of governors. Each of the elected directors has a voting power resembling the total number of votes that the governor gives him, since each governor gives one of the elected directors the voting power which his country represents. The voting power of each governor, as was pointed out earlier, depends upon the amount of financial contribution his country makes to the total capital of the Arab Fund. The quorum of the board of directors is attained when directors representing two-thirds of the total number of votes are present. The decisions of the board of directors are reached by a majority vote except in those cases wherein the Articles of Agreement specify otherwise. Each director casts one vote in reaching a decision, which is different from the case of the board of governors, where each governor casts the number of votes his country holds.

The President

The board of governors appoints a president and a vice-president for the Arab Fund. The president chairs the board of directors and

heads the employees of the Arab Fund. Although the president chairs
the meetings of the board of directors, he does not vote on its decisions
except in cases when the votes are equally divided. In such a case the
president can cast a vote making a decision possible. The president
attends the meetings of the board of governors and takes part in the
deliberations but has no voting rights.

It was noted that in the arrangements of multinational organizations of this type, "the President emerges as the key figure" (White
1974, p. 51). This is true, for example, in the case of the World Bank.
The president in such an organizational arrangement could have a remarkable influence on the way an institution is staffed and operated.
The president of the Arab Fund has the right to hire and fire the experts and the rest of the employees in the framework of personnel regulations approved by the board of governors.

Internal Organization of the Arab Fund

Unlike the Kuwait Fund, the Arab Fund has an elaborate internal
organizational structure that was approved by the board of governors.
It is clear to anyone who raises organizational questions in studying
the Kuwait Fund and the Arab Fund, that both operate with contrasting
organizational doctrines. While the Kuwait Fund maintains a very loose
organizational structure with a minimum specification of responsibilities, authorities, and functions, the Arab Fund maintains an organizational chart that was established as soon as it opened its doors for
business. While the use of "task teams" is the way the Kuwait Fund
does its work, the Arab Fund has a defined departmental structure
with specific functions for each unit.

According to information taken from the Arab Fund in April 1974,
the technical staff (the professional staff in our definition) of the Arab
Fund, as of September 1973, were 16 distributed as follows:

	Actual September 1973	Projected 1974
Technical consultant	1	1
Consultant	2	2
Internal audit	—	1
Finance department	2	4
Administration department	1	3
Program department	2	5
Project department	4	5
Legal department	4	5
Total	16	26

FIGURE 4.1

The Arab Fund Organizational Chart (1973)

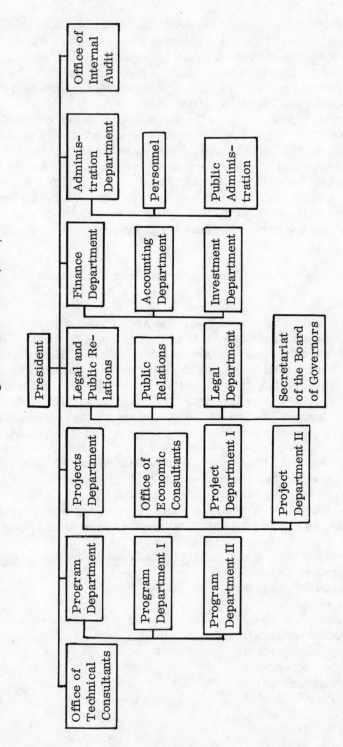

In the initial stage of operations, the Arab Fund depends on a handful of technical consultants who are recruited from international organizations such as the World Bank and the International Monetary Fund for a short period to help in designing lending policies for the Arab Fund and make them operational. In the following we shall describe the activities of the established offices and departments of the Arab Fund. This description depends entirely upon written documents made available to this writer while in Kuwait in 1974.

Office of Technical Consultants

The functions of the technical consultants office include:

- Giving recommendations regarding lending policy and principles and guidelines for project appraisal.
- Counciling the president of the Arab Fund on how the programs and projects departments may conduct their business.
- Giving advice to interested member countries regarding their economic policies in general, and sectoral policies in particular.
- Giving advice on lending operations of the Arab Fund, and the various technical matters that arise during the normal conduct of business.
- Undertaking any other responsibilities assigned to the office by the president of the Arab Fund.

The Programs Department

The programs department is established to handle the following activities:

- Survey international economic and social developments and determine their impact on the member countries.
- Evaluate the economic capabilities of the member countries by studying their development programs and problems of implementation of such programs.
- Suggest aid programs to member countries, based on the result of the two above-mentioned activities.
- Formulate loan policies, programs, and priorities.
- Formulate technical assistance policies, programs, and priorities.
- Study economic problems related to the Arab Fund activities, and design possible solutions on both long-term and short-term bases.

- Study the operations of the international and regional institutions doing similar work in the region in order to recommend means of coordinating the Arab Fund's work with such institutions.
- Design future plans for the Arab Fund in the various spheres of activities in which the Fund is involved.
- Prepare reports on the economies of various member countries.
- In cooperation with the project department, prepare a lending program for each member country that includes sectoral priorities.
- Examine loan applications and prepare negotiation principles that the Arab Fund should observe in collaborating with other public and private lenders who extend loans to member countries.
- Undertake preinvestment studies, and gather relevant information concerning certain projects that the project department is evaluating.
- Participate in negotiating Arab Fund loans.
- Follow on the implementation of the loan agreements, especially in terms of coordinating the activities of the various departments of the Arab Fund as they relate to the implementation of a loan agreement.
- Consult with international and regional agencies working in the field of economic and social development, in order to ensure more effective utilization of international economic assistance to the member countries.

The Projects Department

The projects department is supposed to undertake the following activities:

- Prepare studies of the various sectors of the economy of member countries in order to be able to identify project priorities for each country.
- Undertake the responsibilities related to technical assistance, especially in preparing financial and administrative arrangements for the Fund's missions and the choice of technical experts and consultants for such missions, whether or not these experts are available from the Fund's staff.
- Assist member countries that lack the necessary expertise in preparing project proposals that are later submitted to the Fund for consideration.
- Appraise project proposals submitted to the Arab Fund.
- Recommend the amount of loans, terms of lending, and methods of repayment of loans for the Arab Fund financed projects.

- Ensure that the quality of goods and services that are purchased by the borrower meet the specifications required for the completion of the project.
- Supervise the implementation of Arab Fund projects and recommend methods for overcoming implementation problems.
- Survey the state of affairs of development-financing institutions in the member countries, to recommend means of cooperation between the Arab Fund and such institutions.
- Evaluate the managerial aspects of development-financing institutions in member countries, and assist such institutions in setting up effective organizations and supplying them with managerial talents.
- Cooperate with international and regional agencies in planning and implementing joint projects.
- Study any suggestions presented to the Arab Fund concerning the establishment of a new development institution on a country or regional level, or the reorganization of an existing one. The projects department will then prepare a plan for implementing such suggestions and supervise the implementation.
- Participate in the Arab Fund loan negotiations.

The projects department is divided into two sections, the office of economic consultants and the projects section. During the first two years of operation, the office of economic consultants played a more important role in both formulating ideas and deciding on project financing. The project section is a study unit that undertakes whatever the consultants require in the process of project appraisal.

Organizational Dynamics in the Arab Fund

The Arab Fund offers a contrasting image to that of the Kuwait Fund in terms of its organizational ideology and dynamics. As a multinational organization, its structural arrangements are very elaborate and it has to be approved by its managing boards. Before the Arab Fund was able to do any serious work, it had to have its organizational structure, regulations concerning financial operations, and investment policy guidelines approved by the board of governors.

It seems that the Arab Fund has a major need to "differentiate itself from the institution which was primarily responsible for its creation, i.e. the Kuwait Fund" (White 1974, p. 48). This need is quite understandable in policy terms since the Arab Fund is supposed to give more attention to regional projects and activities vis-a-vis country projects which have constituted most of the work of the Kuwait Fund. The need to differentiate itself from the Kuwait Fund has affected the

Arab Fund not only in policy terms but also in terms of organizational doctrine and dynamics. To start a recruitment policy different from that of the Kuwait Fund, the Arab Fund hired a consulting firm to identify professionally qualified Arabs working abroad. The consulting firm produced a list of 500 individuals who were asked if they were interested in joining the Arab Fund. Likely applicants were flown to Kuwait to be interviewed (White 1974, p. 51).

On appearance, at least, this recruitment practice is different from methods of recruitment used by the Kuwait Fund. Such recruitment methods used by the Arab Fund would have led to the formation of a group of professionals who would be hired to fit in an organization devoted to a clear regional development goal. In practice, recruitment was much influenced by personal considerations, and avowed regional goals as criteria for recruitment were submerged under the influence of other factors.

The Arab Fund depended on a small number of key consultants, seconded from such institutions as the World Bank, the International Monetary Fund and the United Nations. These consultants played a prominent role in deciding what kind of professionals needed to be hired (for example engineers, economists, financial analysts and so on), and who will be hired. The most decisive element in shaping recruitment, however, was the president of the Arab Fund, who holds the formal authority in relation to staffing the Fund. The president was influenced by the consultant's views and their personal preferences. The outcome of the recruitment method was similar to the Kuwait Fund pattern of recruitment in terms of the dominance of personal considerations. Yet, the difference is that, while in the case of the Kuwait Fund recruitment, authority resides in a single figure without much pressure on him, in the case of the Arab Fund the authorized recruiter is under the strong influence of senior consultants within the Arab Fund, and outside pressure from governments who want a fair representation of their countries among the Fund's staff.

In similar situations to that of the Arab Fund, factions usually develop and the outcome of such a recruitment pattern may not be conducive to smooth intraorganizational cooperation. For example, the project department in the Arab Fund (as of April 1974), consisted of eight engineers, one economist, and two financial analysts. The strong representation of engineers was not particularly welcomed by the economist and the financial analysts. They believed it detrimental to a sound project appraisal process. This overemphasis on engineers was seen to be the result of the influence of one of the technical consultants (an engineer himself), on the recruitment pattern of the Arab Fund.

In studying the decision-making process in the Arab Fund, this writer was faced with some difficulties. In the case of the Kuwait Fund, interviews were used to supplement a participant observation method.

In the case of the Arab Fund, participant observation was not possible (or, at least, not for sufficient duration to make the method worthwhile). Interviews with influential decision makers were not granted. In such a multinational institution as the Arab Fund, where employees are prohibited by regulations from discussing any aspects of the Fund's work without the permission of the authorities (Article (5) of the personnel regulations of the Arab Fund), gathering enough information on decision making proved to be an awfully difficult task. There was also a prevalent attitude among the staff members to avoid talking about anything that could be interpreted as reflecting views on such issues as Arab regional cooperation or inter-Arab politics.

In discussing decision making in the Arab Fund this writer had to depend on sporadically gathered information and personal impressions which were gained through several visits to the Arab Fund and discussions with its staff. The decision-making process in the Arab Fund is influenced by two elements: the formal authorities ascribed to the various roles (for example, the heads of departments and the president); and the personalities of the participants. According to available information that one can gather regarding decision making, it seems that formal and real authority concerning final decisions fall in the hands of the president. He has enough personal stature to bolster his formal authority and to translate this authority into actual decisions. The influences upon him, however, come from technical consultants who affect decision outcomes not only by means of the technical expertise they have, but also through their personal influence on the president. In describing the recruitment aspect of the Arab Fund personnel policies, we mentioned the possibilities of the development of factions among members of the staff. Although it cannot be proved empirically on the basis of the little information available, there is a real possibility that informal leaders for certain groups could develop within the organization. The loyalty of those leaders could still be to the president of the Arab Fund, but they would try to compete with each other in influencing the president's decisions, which would affect the limited welfare of their groups. The influence of such informal factional leaders may not be directed toward major policy decisions of the Arab Fund, which are subject to serious considerations in the board of governors meetings, but they could try to influence such issues as new recruitment to the professional staff, formation of the Arab Fund loan missions to Arab countries, assignment of consulting contracts in Fund-financed projects and others.

In describing the various activities of the different departments of the Arab Fund, it was clear that such ambitious undertakings could not be done with such a small staff as the Arab Fund has. It is also important to note that dependence on technical consultants seconded from the International Monetary Fund and the World Bank is a temporary phase in Arab Fund development. The impressions gained on the present decision-making practices, which induce us to believe in the possibility of developing a factional structure within the Arab Fund affecting its decision making, could be indicative of only a passing phase in the development of the Arab Fund. A firmer view of how decision making will develop depends on what lines of development the Arab Fund will follow in terms of recruiting permanent staff and developing its own corps of senior staff who will replace the present technical consultants in playing a major role in decisions.

THE ARAB FUND: POLICIES AND OPERATIONS

The main policy rationale behind establishing the Arab Fund is to promote regional cooperation by creating a "motivating force that will assist the Arab World in achieving the basic tasks" needed for economic and social development (Al-Atiqui 1973, p. 2). In that sense, the Arab Fund is designed to pursue policies that are regional in nature, acknowledging that other national institutions, such as the Kuwait Fund, are inherently limited in handling regional tasks.

It is rather premature to make judgments concerning the policies and operations of the Arab Fund since it is in the early stages of its development. It is worthwhile, however, to comment on what has already been done and to speculate on what lines of development the Arab Fund might pursue.

On February 7, 1974, the president of the Arab Fund held a news conference on the occasion of signing three agreements involving loans to three Arab countries: the People's Democratic Republic of Yemen (South Yemen), Syria, and Tunisia.

The first loan was for a multi-purpose project to be established in the Mikla area in South Yemen. The project was designed to increase fishing activities and improve South Yemen's capabilities to export seafood. The amount of the loan was KD 3.2 million with 4 percent interest to be repayed over 20 years with a five-year grace period.

The second loan was in the amount of KD 2 million to Syria with 5 percent interest and a 20-year maturation period of which five years are grace period. The loan was given to enable Syria to build storages for oil by-products.

The third loan was given to Tunisia in the amount of KD 3 million for an electricity generation project. The terms of the loan included 6 percent and a 20-year maturation with a grace period of five years.

According to more recent information, the Arab Fund has concluded 10 loan agreements with eight Arab countries since it started its operations in 1973 (As-Siassa, 6 February 1975).

It is not difficult to see why the Arab Fund's operations have been in the conventional style of country-project lending. Since the need for such type of lending is still prevalent in the Arab countries, the Arab Fund will always receive loan applications from various Arab countries to finance country projects. In terms of such aspects as project perception, selection, and appraisal, country projects are easier to handle by a financial institution than integration or regional projects.

When the Arab Fund Articles of Agreement were debated, there was a chance to insist on describing the Fund's operations, on its involvement only in those projects, or other activities that could be termed regional. Rather, broad instruction was given to the Arab Fund management to give "priority to vital and inter-Arab projects." (Articles of Agreement, Article 2).

After the Arab Fund was created, a need was felt by its management to "achieve." Since the board of governors meets annually, this need to achieve meant that in the coming annual meeting something substantial had to be presented to the board of governors in the form of concluded loan agreements. The fact that there is a disguised competition between the Arab Fund and the Kuwait Fund is not questioned by most of the informed Arab development experts. This competition does not have serious negative implications; or, more significantly, it does not hinder cooperation among the two Funds. Nevertheless, this competition is partly the reason behind the need felt by the Arab Fund management to come up with concluded loan agreements to be presented in the annual meeting of the board of governors. It also affects the Arab Fund assignment of priorities among its various activities, to the effect that those activities which require less time and effort and produce presentable results (such as concluding loan agreements), are given priority over the more demanding activities of studying and preparing integration projects or regional cooperation schemes.

To be able to come up with seriously formulated regional projects, the Arab Fund has to put more time and effort into studying such projects. This means that it will not be able to get as many loan agreements involving country projects as it is doing now. An entrepreneurial and innovative role by the Arab Fund in the field of integration projects could be very significant for better Arab cooperation schemes. To be able to perform such a role, however, the Arab Fund management needs to perceive its role from a different perspective. To be able to do serious work in integration projects, the Arab Fund would have to sacrifice other activities such as country-project financing, which could be done by such national institutions as the Kuwait Fund, the Abu-Dhabi Fund, the Iraq Fund, and the Saudi Fund. The last two funds are recent creations and they signal the availability of new resources for country-project financing in the Arab world.

What the Arab Fund has been doing in the last two years is not in total harmony with the policy statements made for it by its governors. During the 1973 meeting of the board of governors, the chairman of the board of governors identified three main tasks for the newly established Arab Fund: first, the entrepreneurial task of finding and promoting mutually beneficial opportunities for cooperation; second, the task of providing a focal point for attracting Arab development expertise working outside the Arab world; third, the brokerage task of finding and promoting opportunities in the Arab region for the investment of surplus Arab funds (Al-Atiqui 1973).

We mentioned earlier that in institutions like the Arab Fund, the board of governors is not usually the policy-formulator organ, although it might be the policy-legitimizer organ. If the actual policies and operations of the Arab Fund truly reflected the policy statements of the chairman of the board of governors, the lines of evolution of the Arab Fund would be a little different from what they are now.

During the early months of 1974 the Arab Fund commissioned a study of road communication systems among the Arab countries. This study was to produce a scheme for improving inter-Arab transportation systems. Although we have no definite information about the results of this specific study, we are sure that it did not materialize as an actual Arab Fund project until February 1975.

The Arab Fund cannot be blamed for doing what it did (that is, becoming involved in country projects), but for what it did not do (embarking on a truly innovative approach to regional and integrative projects and programs). There are some elements in the Arab Fund guidelines of operations which indicate a basic commitment to Arab cooperation. Arab bidders in the Arab Fund-financed projects are given certain preference. For example, if the quality of goods and services offered by Arab bidders are similar to those of foreign bidders, Arab bidders are given the preference even if their bids are 15 percent higher in price than foreign bidders. Arab consulting firms are given preference over similar quality firms in the Arab Fund-financed projects. These stipulations were included in "Articles of Policies on Lending and Borrowing," approved by the board of directors of the Arab Fund in 1974.

The significant question for the Arab Fund now is whether or not it will be able to perform an innovative and entrepreneurial role in furthering Arab regional cooperation and integration. If the Arab Fund loses the opportunity to perform such a role, and continues to perform similar functions to those of the Kuwait Fund or Abu-Dhabi Fund, its contribution to Arab regional development will be insignificant. The Arab Fund does not have the resources available to the Kuwait Fund, and lacks the organizational dynamism that the Kuwait Fund methods of operations offer. We mentioned earlier that we can only comment on the Arab Fund lines of development as seen from its operations in the last two years; it is too early to offer conclusive evidence concerning the Arab Fund future development. Yet, in order for the Arab Fund to serve Arab economic integration, a reevaluation of its operational policies needs to be undertaken immediately in order to gear its future operations toward the broad policy goals that the Arab Fund was established to fulfill.

5

This study demonstrates that the Kuwait Fund is an effective organization in attaining both explicit (official) and implicit (operative) goals. Two types of measurement are employed to assess effectiveness, objective and subjective. Objective measurement includes such indicators of effectiveness as can be used to compare the Fund's performance with similar institutions: volume of lending, percentage of disbursements to total loan commitments, and percentage of administrative expenses to volume of operations. Subjective indicators of effectiveness are based on the views, held by various actors interested in the work of the Fund, regarding its effectiveness. In this category we include the views of political rulers of Kuwait, the Kuwait Fund management, and World Bank officials who have dealt with the Fund on various occasions.

Objective indicators suggest that the Fund is an effective organization.* According to the subjective indicators the Fund is likewise effective. First, we can take the Kuwait government's decision to raise the capital of the Fund and expand its operations as an indicator of effectiveness.† Second, the Fund management perceive their institution as an effective organization. Third, the World Bank officials who are in contact with the Kuwait Fund have high regard for the Fund's work and quality of performance.‡

---

*See Chapter 3, pp. 61-63.

†See Chapter 2, p. 20.

‡Their views were expressed to this writer during formal interviews in August 1974, in which the Fund's performance in the field of Arab development financing was perceived to be of high quality.

It is interesting to compare the organizational image of the Kuwait Fund with the model of an effective organization derived from Western industrial settings (Price 1968). Price's inventory of organizational effectiveness is based on a review of 50 organizational studies dealing with effectiveness. When information on effectiveness was not available, Price used productivity, conformity, morale, adaptiveness, and institutionalization as intervening variables that were regarded as having a positive relationship to effectiveness (Price 1968, p. 7).

An effective organization, according to Price tends to have the following:

- A high degree of division of labor;
- a high degree of legitimacy;
- a rational legal type of decision making;
- the maximum degree of centralization with respect to strategic decisions;
- a high degree of autonomy;
- an ideology;
- a high degree of cooptation;
- a high degree of representation*; and
- a high degree of vertical and/or horizontal communication.

Organizationally, the Kuwait Fund has some characteristics which coincide with this; but many do not. The Kuwait Fund does not have a high degree of division of labor, nor does it have a rational legal type of decision making.

We consider the degree of division of labor in the Fund and its decision-making system as two important aspects of its organizational dynamics. Under conditions that prevailed during the last decade the Fund proved to be an effective organization. Yet, when we discussed the impact of expansion on the Fund's organization, we indicated the need for a higher degree of division of labor within the Fund, together with a more precise definition of authority for individuals who hold decision-making roles. Propositions included in Price's inventory model appear to be relevant for large complex organizations. Indeed, when the Fund expands it will have to come closer to a bureaucratic structure in order to meet the huge work volume concomitant with expansion.

This study aimed at answering some questions related to theory and policy of development organizations. From a theory point of view, it was demonstrated that a goal-, action-oriented approach can be

---

*Representation is defined as "the practice of a social system's members joining other social systems with the goal of increasing its institutionalization" (Price 1968, p. 116).

illuminating in the study of development organizations. Such an approach permits students of organization theory to grasp the organizational dynamics in such a way that both micro- and macro-issues can be tackled and explained. In the case of the Kuwait Fund, we believe we were able to show how and why the organization was created, and to explain its development in a satisfactory way by concentrating on a goal context for the organization.

We hope to have demonstrated the policy relevance of a goal-action model in organizational studies. Applying such a model to the Fund, it was feasible to explain the policy developments that took place, especially the drastic expansion in the Fund's resources and geographical domain of operations. We indicated that the Kuwait government's decision to increase the resources of the Kuwait Fund and to allow it to operate in all Third World countries was a result of its demonstrated effectiveness in meeting the first set of goals, legitimizing Kuwait's independence and enhancing its image as a responsible state in the Arab region.

The Kuwait Fund has already started its operations in non-Arab countries. During April 1975, a mission of the Fund headed by the director general visited the Philippines, Malaysia, and Thailand to look into possibilities of aid to those countries (As-Siassa, 2 April 1975).

In the introduction, we mentioned an implicit question that was kept in mind throughout the study: what role does the Kuwait Fund play in promoting Arab regional development and integration and how can this role be furthered? The study argues that the major goal of the Fund is not promoting Arab regional integration. As a Kuwaiti institution, the paramount concern of the Fund is limited by the interests of Kuwait. The Fund performs a political role in the context of Kuwait government policies in the Arab region. This is not to say, however, that the Fund does not play a significant role in promoting Arab regional integration. For more than one reason, the Kuwait Fund performs an important role in promoting Arab economic cooperation and integration. The Kuwait government realizes that it has a major commitment to other Arab countries who need Kuwait aid. The moral obligation for assistance to needy Arab countries is a factor that will always influence Kuwait decisions regarding inter-Arab cooperation and development. The oil era in Kuwait is not everlasting; therefore, in the minds of the Fund management, aid commitments to the Arab countries will come before any other commitments of aid the Kuwait Fund may make (As-Siassa, 24 April 1975).

The question of what will happen when Kuwait's oil wells are depleted must constantly be in the minds of Kuwait rulers when they take an active role in extending aid and promoting economic cooperation in the Arab region. When the oil is gone, it will be in the interest of

Kuwait to be integrated economically into a larger interdependent Arab economy. The facts about Kuwait's self-interest are only part of the aid issue. Many people whom this author met in the Fund are honest believers in the common fate of the Arab region.

The moral and political grounds for Kuwait Fund's role in promoting Arab integration do not make it the most powerful instrument of Arab economic integration. The need for multicountry institutions such as the Arab Fund is obvious. Such institutions combine political will and economic resources that could concentrate exclusively on those aspects that are integrative in nature. It is unfortunate that, in policy terms, the Articles of Agreement of the Arab Fund did not require it to be an exclusive instrument for the integration of the Arab economies. The Arab Fund management, however, has an opportunity to make of the Fund a true integrative institution by concentrating on such activities that further Arab integration. If this opportunity is not immediately exploited, the Arab Fund will continue to perform a marginal economic role as a financier of some scattered country projects in the Arab region.

Dear Mr. _____

    This questionnaire is intended as a survey of the opinions and attitudes of the Fund's professional staff and top management. It touches upon subjects related to the work of the Fund and its Arab character. In some cases I had to structure the response according to some choices. These choices are mainly for classification purposes and statistical analysis and I hope you will not find them too imposing I hope that answering this questionnaire will not cause you any inconvenience.

    Your cooperation is much appreciated and your comments would be most valued.

    Thank you.

Soliman Demir.

a) Name: b) Age
c) Nationality: d) Place of birth
e) Present job:
f) Education (list degrees starting with B.A. or equivalent)

g) Previous jobs (start with the most recent)

1) Why did you join the Fund?

2) What is in your judgment the closest Arab country to Kuwait, culturally?

3) From a political perspective, what is the Arab country closest to Kuwait?

4) Which of these two problems do you think to be the basic one facing the Arabs: (make a choice)

    Israel _____   Underdevelopment _____
           _____   _____

5) Do you believe that economic integration in the Arab world is
   a) a possibility that could be worked out if the Arabs are interested enough? _____
   _____

   b) a far reaching goal that requires many changes in the structure of Arab economies which could take a very long time? _____
   _____

   c) an urgent necessity for the sake of more rapid development in the Arab world? _____
   _____

6) Which of these statements do you accept as describing the relationship between economic unity and political unity in the Arab world? (Please choose one)

   a) economic unity is easier to achieve than political unity _____
   _____

b) political unity is easier to achieve than economic unity _____

c) economic unity and political unity in the Arab world _____
   are inseparable and achieving one would entail the other

7) Are you satisfied with the present level of economic cooperation among Arab countries?

very satisfied ____   moderately satisfied ____   dissatisfied ____

8) How do you judge the oil-rich countries' contribution to Arab development?

generous ____   enough ____   less than enough ____

9) Did some oil countries, in your opinion, contribute more than others to the cause of Arab development?

Yes ____   No ____   Don't know ____

If the answer is 'yes'

10) What are these countries?

11) Do you think there is any obligation on the capital-rich countries in the Arab World to aid the capital-poor ones?

Yes ____   No ____   Undecided ____

12) In what way, if any, could the capital-surplus countries contribute more to Arab regional development? Please be as specific as possible.

13) If we define democracy in the Western tradition (which means that France, England, West Germany and the United States are democracies), do you believe that democracy is the best political system for the Arabs?

Yes ____   No ____   Undecided ____

14) In your opinion, which of the following Arab countries are closer to socialism and which are closer to capitalism? (indicate socialism with 'S' and capitalism with 'C')

Iraq _____	Saudi Arabia _____
Egypt _____	Algeria _____
Sudan _____	Kuwait _____
Jordan _____	Syria _____

15) The majority of the people (that is, the masses) have the best human conditions in:

| Yugoslavia _____ | United States _____ |
| Soviet Union _____ | China _____ |

16) What is the Arab country that comes closer than any other Arab country in taking care of the interests of its masses?

17) If you were given your present income doing a similar job, what Arab country (other than Kuwait) would you choose to live and work in for the rest of your life?

18) If the answer for the previous question is your home country give another preference.

19) Which of the following statements seems to you to be a correct description of Arab unity:

a) Arab unity is a romantic dream of the past but is not likely to come again in the future. _____

b) Arab unity is a distant goal in the future that could be achieved if the various Arab countries planned carefully to reduce differences in political, economic, and social conditions prevailing in various Arab countries. _____

c) Arab unity is a definite policy goal that can be realized in the near future if Arab leaders are sincere about it. _____

20) Which of the following Arab leaders comes closer to your image of a leader who believe(d) in Arab nationalism and cooperation?

Nasser _____   Sadat _____   Faisal _____   Assad _____

Bakr _____   Boumedien _____   Quaddafi _____   Hassan II _____

21) Which of the following leaders pursue(d) policies that were closer to Arab nationalism and achievement of closer Arab cooperation?

Nasser _____   Sadat _____   Faisal _____   Assad _____

Bakr _____   Boumedien _____   Quaddafi _____   Hassan II _____

22) After the 1967 war there have been many political and intellectual dialogues in the Arab world about the reasons for the defeat and the road to victory. I will give you a sample of three trends to choose the one you find most agreeable to you. (Please make one choice)

a) a secular-liberal trend represented by Dr. Constantine Zuraik who sees the reasons for the defeat in Arab cultural and techno-logical backwardness. The road to victory is to become more modern in the Western sense: to absorb Western technology and social values, to industrialize, to separate state from re-ligion and so on. _____

b) an Islamic-religious trend represented by Dr. Salah Eddin El-Munajjid who sees the reasons for the defeat in the decay of religion and decline of Islam in the Arab world. Going back to the basic and true teachings of Islam would give the Arabs a new sense of courage and dignity which would be the road to victory. _____

c) a revolutionary socialist trend represented by Dr. Sedek Jalal Al-Azm who sees the defeat as a natural outcome of the decay of traditional bourgeois Arab regimes. The road to victory would be a revolution of scientific socialism that does away with all the existing methods of social organization and production and brings about a new way of life based on a new ideology of man and science. _____

_____

23) In what way do you perceive national development? (choose one)
   a) as an economic concept   ____
   b) as a political concept   ____
   c) as a sociological concept   ____
   d) as a concept composed of all the previous elements   ____

24) Success of national development depends on the following conditions (please arrange in order of importance)
   a) good political system   ____
   b) good planning models and well thought through plans   ____
   c) good administrative system   ____
   d) other important factors:

25) The best way to develop a country like the Sudan is to give priority to
   a) education, health and family planning   ____
   b) industries and productive activities   ____
   c) other fields: ____

26) In the Arab countries, generally, the social projects such as education and health are difficult to finance because of a lack of interest on the part of funding institutions:

Agree _____   Disagree _____   Undecided _____

27) It is difficult, in the present development of the cost/benefit analysis to measure satisfactorily and with precision the benefit of such social projects as education, health care, and family planning

Agree _____   Disagree _____   Undecided _____

28) The difficulty in measuring the benefits of social projects is
   a) a major reason for the difficulty to get it financed   ____
   b) a minor reason for the difficulty to get it financed   ____
   c) has no connection with the difficulty to get social
      projects financed.   ____

29) Private business is more efficient than public enterprise because the profit motive induces efficiency.

Agree _____   Disagree _____   Undecided _____

30) Efficiency should be the prime goal of any government interested in promoting development.

Agree _____   Disagree _____   Undecided _____

31) If you were asked to generalize from your experience and knowledge of the Arab countries, what would they need most to improve their conditions? (please choose one)

a) good and devoted political leaders who give high priority ____
   to development and make the necessary sacrifices   ____

b) good planners and economists who would set up economically sound plans that will help the country achieve
   development   ____

c) good managers and administrators who would turn even   ____
   modest plans into success   ____

32) The discipline of economics has progressed in the last decade because

a) it has become more mathematically oriented and rigorous. ____

b) it has improved communications and understanding with
   other social sciences such as sociology and political
   science.   ____

c) other

33) Give the name of one or two economists in the field of development whom you think have made lasting contributions to the field to understand its complexity. (You need not answer if you don't consider yourself an economist).

34) If experts on politics were included on the planning boards or councils in the Arab countries do you think they would make the work of these boards:

    a) more tedious, time consuming, and less efficient   _____

    b) more relevant to the social realities of development   _____

    c) they would not make any difference   _____

35) If experts on administration and management were included on the planning boards or councils in the Arab countries do you think they would make the work of these boards:

    a) more tedious, time consuming and less efficient   _____

    b) more relevant to the social realities of development   _____

    c) they would not make any difference   _____

36) If experts on sociology were included on the planning board or councils in the Arab world do you think they would make the work of these boards:

    a) more tedious, time consuming, and less efficient   _____

    b) more relevant to the social realities of development   _____

    c) they would not make any difference   _____

37) Give me the name of three works that you consider to be very important for anyone who works in the field of development. You can cite works by writers in any field of knowledge (that is, social science, pure sciences, philosophy, literature, and history), Arabs or foreigners.

    __

    __

    __

Comments:

Dear Mr.

The aim of this Delphi exercise is to reach a consensus of expert opinion regarding the future image for the Kuwait Fund. This intellectual exercise is a substitute for empirical evidence which we could not have since we are looking into the future.

In responding to the various points please try to be as objective as you can. Try to make your own preferences of no effect on your projections for the future.

Since this exercise deals with future orientations, it is open to many weaknesses, the most prominent of which is uncertainty. I suggest that in projecting the images of the future you make use of past trends as guidelines, but more important will be your own evaluation of the proportionate importance of the various variables that you think will have a dominant effect on determining the future.

In responding to each question try to look ten years ahead so the outcome of this exercise may be termed as your own tentative image of KF in 1985.

The time you take responding to these questions will further a scientific undertaking for which I am personally thankful, and will, hopefully, be of value to the KF.

N.B.: I would appreciate it if you would answer on a separate sheet of paper those questions which you think need more elaborate answers.

I. ARAB REGIONAL DEVELOPMENT

1. Which of the Arab countries would forward the industrialization base for Arab development?

2. Do you expect oil countries to concentrate on building industrial bases at home?

3. Give a possible scenario for the case of a successful economic integration in the Arab countries and another scenario for a case of unsuccessful economic integration.

4. How do you think the following factors would contribute (either positively or negatively) to Arab regional development? a) fall of oil revenues as a result of technical-political measures on the part of consuming nations; b) economic competition among Arab countries.

5. From an institutional point of view, what do you think would be the most successful means of enhancing regional cooperation: multilateral channels—bilateral means—national institutions with regional functions (possibly KF, Abu-Dhabi Fund)?

6. Would you expect KF to work out a regional plan for the area and begin soliciting loan applications according to this plan which has been set up on a regional basis?

7. Would you expect KF to work as a consultant to Kuwait's private capital concerning investment opportunities in the Arab world?

8. Do you expect KF to borrow from the capital market in Kuwait and invest in other Arab countries; if so under what conditions?

9. Do you expect a change in KF's policies concerning various types of aid (that is, more concentration on grants, technical assistance and interest free loans than was the policy in the past)?

II. KF DEVELOPMENT PERSPECTIVES

1. Do you expect the Fund to get involved in the social aspects of development?

2. How do you think the Fund would operate in terms of a development policy for the Arab countries?

3. Do you expect the development of an interest in social equality that would guide KF's operations in the borrowing countries?

III. ORGANIZATION OF KF:

In the process of expansion KF would have to undergo some modifications in its present organizational structure. I will mention some of the points that you might think important in a new organizational frame for KF. In projecting a future organizational structure you are welcome to suggest other elements not mentioned here.

The elements that could obviously be subject to modification with the expansion of KF are:

1. An increase in staff number and specialities.

2. Departmental reorganization and structure.

3. The methods of operations in the Fund especially as regards:

   a) a more elaborate authority structure

   b) a more defined task specification especially for the professional staff.

   c) a more routine operational definition of loan processing beginning with loan applications, loan investigation, decision, and loan service.

AGREEMENT ESTABLISHING THE ARAB FUND
FOR ECONOMIC AND SOCIAL DEVELOPMENT*

The Governments of:
    The Hashimite Kingdom of Jordan
    The Republic of Tunisia
    The Algerian Democratic and People's Republic
    The Democratic Republic of the Sudan
    The Republic of Iraq
    The Kingdom of Saudi Arabia
    The Syrian Arab Republic
    The Lybian Arab Republic
    The Arab Republic of Egypt
    The Yemen Arab Republic
    The State of Kuwait
    The Republic of Lebanon
    The Kingdom of Morocco
    The People's Democratic Republic of Yemen
    The State of the United Arab Emirates
    The State of Bahrain
    The State of Qatar

Desirous of building the Arab Economy on a strong foundation that will enable it to meet the requirements of economic and social development in their countries, and in order to achieve the aims of the Pact of the League of Arab States.

Have approved the text of this Agreement as adopted by the Economic Council in its resolution Number 345 at its meeting held on Thursday, 18th Safar, 1388H., (16th May, 1968).

Article 1   There shall be established an Arab regional financial organization, enjoying an independent juridical personality, called the "ARAB

---

*Updated as of October 30, 1974.

FUND FOR ECONOMIC AND SOCIAL DEVEL-
OPMENT", and having its Head Office in the
City of Kuwait. The Fund may, by a decision
of the Board of Governors as provided for in
Article 19, establish branches and agencies
in any country.

PART ONE: PURPOSES OF THE FUND

Article 2

The Fund shall participate in the financing of
economic and social development projects in
the Arab states and countries by:
1 Financing economic projects of an investment character by means of loans granted on
easy terms to Governments, and to public or
private organizations and institutions, giving
preference to economic projects that are vital
to the Arab entity and to joint Arab projects.
2 Encouraging, directly or indirectly, the
investment of public and private capital in
such a manner as to ensure the development
and growth of the Arab economy.
3 Providing technical expertise and assistance
in the various fields of economic development.

PART TWO: MEMBERSHIP AND CAPITAL

Article 3

Members of the Fund shall be:
1 Member States of the League of Arab States
and other Arab countries having subscribed
to the capital of the Fund before the 1st of
July 1968. These shall be considered as
founding members.
2 Any other Arab states or countries whose
accession to the Agreement shall be approved
by the Board of Governors.

Article 4

The Board of Governors of the Fund may decide to accept the participation of public and
private Arab financial institutions and organizations in the Arab states and countries in the
capital of the Fund.

Article 5

1 The capital of this Fund shall be One Hundred Million Kuwaiti Dinars (One Kuwaiti dinar being equal to 2.48828 grams of gold) that are convertible into convertible currencies.

2 The capital shall be divided into ten thousand shares having a value of Ten Thousand Kuwaiti Dinars each.*

3 Upon signing this Agreement, the founding members shall subscribe shares of the capital of the Fund in accordance with the following schedule:

State	Number of Shares
The Hashimite Kingdom of Jordan	200
The Republic of Tunisia	50
The Algerian Democratic and People's Republic	400
The Democratic Republic of the Sudan	150
The Republic of Iraq	750
The Kingdom of Saudi Arabia	1880
The Syrian Arab Republic	300
The Lybian Arab Republic	1200
The Arab Republic of Egypt	1050
The Yemen Arab Republic	50
The State of Kuwait	3000
The Republic of Lebanon	100
The Kingdom of Morocco	200
The People's Democratic Republic of Yemen	1
The State of The United Arab Emirates	500
The State of Bahrain	50
The State of Qatar	100
The Somali Democratic Republic	5
The Islamic Republic of Mauritania	10
The Sultanate of Oman	204

Article 6
Increase of Capital

The capital of the Fund may be increased on the following conditions:

1 The approval by an absolute majority of the votes cast in the case of issuing new shares

---

*The capital of the Fund has become 102 Million Kuwaiti dinars by issuing 200 new shares to cover the subscription of the Sultanate of Oman.

for allocation to an Arab country wishing to join the Fund.

2 The approval by a three-fourths majority of the votes cast in all other cases.

3 In case an increase is decided upon pursuant to the preceding paragraph, every member may subscribe thereto in the proportion which its shares bear to the capital and under such conditions as the Board of Governors may decide. The proportion may be increased or reduced, subject to the approval of an absolute majority of the votes cast.

4 Only members of the Fund and institutions and organizations provided for in Article 4 hereof, can subscribe for shares in an increase of capital.

Article 7
Subscription

1 Each founding member shall subscribe shares in accordance with the schedule set forth in paragraph 3 of Article 5. The Board of Governors shall determine the shares to be subscribed by other members in the manner provided for in paragraph 1 of Article 6.

2 Shares shall be issued at their nominal value.

3 The member shall pay 10% of the value of the shares for which it has subscribed upon depositing the instruments of ratification of this Agreement. The member shall deposit such amount in the Fund's name with the Ministry of Finance of the State of Kuwait, which shall invest it under Government guarantee and return it together with the profits accruing therefrom to the body that the Board of Governors of the Fund shall designate at its first meeting.

4 In addition to the stipulations in Paragraph 3, the member shall pay 10% of the value of the shares for which it has subscribed, upon this Agreement coming into force, pursuant to Article 40 hereof.

5 The remaining capital shall be paid up in ten equal annual installments, the first of which shall fall due one year after the Fund shall commence its operations.

6 In case of accession of an Arab state or country to this Agreement after its coming into force, the new member shall pay on the share portion allotted to it, an amount proportionately equal to that paid by existing members on their shares.

Article 8

1 No member shall be deemed liable, by virtue of its membership, for the Fund's obligations beyond the limits set out in this Agreement.

2 Every member shall remain liable for the unpaid portion of its shares.

3 The provisions of Paragraphs 1 and 2 of this Article shall apply to the organizations and institutions provided for in Article 4.

Article 9
Disposal of Shares

Shares in the Fund may not be disposed of in any manner whatsoever, nor may their title be transferred, except to the Fund.

Article 10
Resources of the Fund

1 The Fund's resources shall consist of the capital subscribed, the reserves, and the loans raised by the Fund through the issuing of bonds or the obtaining of credits from public and private Arab institutions or from individuals or international institutions.

2 The Fund shall determine the conditions relating to bonds issue.

3 The value of the bonds issued by the Fund may not, at any time, exceed twice the amount of the capital, unless by special resolution of the Fund's Board of Governors to be adopted by a two-third majority of votes.

PART THREE: FUNCTIONS OF THE FUND

Article 11
Operations of the
Fund

The Fund shall, in particular, carry out the following operations:

1 Borrow funds from internal and foreign markets and determine the guarantee necessary therefor.

2 Guarantee the securities relating to the projects wherein the Fund has invested its resources in order to facilitate their sale.

3 Buy and sell the securities issued or guaranteed by it or wherein it has invested its resources.

4 Invest surplus resources, its savings and pension funds and the like, in first class securities.

5 Carry out any other operation connected with the purposes of the Fund as provided for in Article 2.

**Article 12
Guarantees**

1 All lending operations undertaken by the Fund in favour of a public or private organization or institution shall be guaranteed by the Government of the State or the country where the project is carried out.

2 The Fund is entitled, when financing a non-governmental project, to ask for special guarantees in addition to the governmental guarantees stipulated in Paragraph 1 of this Article.

**Article 13
Limitations of
Financing**

1 The Fund shall not finance a project in the territory of any member without the permission of the government concerned.

2 The Fund shall stipulate that the proceeds of the loan be used for the purposes for which the loan was granted.

3 The Fund shall not share in the management of any project wherein it has invested its resources.

4 The Fund shall carry out its financing operations on the terms it shall deem appropriate, taking into consideration the requirements and risks of the project.

5 The Fund shall ascertain, through its technical experts, the reliability of any project before financing it.

6 The Fund shall strive for the continuous investment of its resources on satisfactory terms.

7 The Fund may raise loans in any member country to finance a project after obtaining the permission of the government of that country. In case the project is to be carried out in the country of another member, the

member in whose country the loan is raised shall undertake to transfer the proceeds of the loan to the country where the project is to be carried out, at the Fund's request.

Article 14
Currencies in which
loans are granted

The Fund shall pay the borrower the amount of the loan in the currency agreed upon by the two parties and as required for the execution of the project.

Article 15
Conversion of
Currencies

The Fund shall be entitled to convert the currencies at its disposal into any other currency deemed best suited for its purposes.

Article 16
Repayment of Loans

Contracts relating to the loans granted by the Fund shall provide for the methods of repayment of such loans as follows:
1 The Fund shall determine the cost of the loans granted by it, the commission, the methods of discharge of the debt, the dates of maturity, the payment, and the conditions relating thereto.
2 The loan contract shall stipulate the currency in which payments due shall be made. The Fund shall endeavour, as far as possible, to recover its loans in the currency in which they were contracted. The borrower may, however, repay the loan in another currency subject to the approval of the Fund.
3 The Fund may modify the terms of the loan contract at the borrower's request, but without prejudice to the interest of the Fund or other members and subject to the approval of the guaranteeing government.
4 The Fund may modify the conditions of repayment of the loan.

Article 17
Prohibition of
Political Activity

The Fund and the officers in charge of its management shall not interfere in political affairs. Economic and social considerations shall be the only relevant factors in the making of decisions.

PART FOUR: ORGANIZATION AND MANAGEMENT

Article 18
Structure of the Fund

The Fund shall be composed of the Board of Governors, the Director-General Chairman of the Board of Directors, the Board of Directors, the Loan Committees, and the staff necessary to perform the duties determined by the Administration of the Fund.

Article 19
Board of Governors

1 The Board of Governors shall consist of a Governor and an Alternate Governor, appointed by each member of the Fund for a period of five years, unless the member considers the replacement of either of them during the said period; they may be reappointed. The Board shall elect every year one of the Governors as its Chairman.
2 The Board of Governors shall be considered as the General Assembly of the Fund, and shall have all powers. It may delegate to the Board of Directors any of its powers, except the power to:

  a Admit new members.
  b Increase the capital.
  c Suspend a member.
  d Settle disputes over the interpretation of the provisions of this Agreement.
  e Conclude agreements for the purpose of cooperating with other international organizations.
  f Terminate the operations of the Fund and liquidate its assets.
  g Determine the distribution of the net income of the Fund.

3 The Board of Governors shall meet once a year at least. It shall also meet whenever so requested by any three of its members having one quarter of the total voting power, or by the Board of Directors.
4 The meeting of the Board shall be valid provided a quorum is present representing no less than two-thirds of the total voting power.

5 The Board of Governors may establish the necessary procedure whereby the Board of Directors may obtain the approval of the members of the Board of Governors on a specific question without calling a meeting of the latter.

6 The Board of Governors and the Board of Directors, each within its province, may lay down such rules, instructions and regulations as may be necessary to conduct the business of the Fund.

7 The Governors and their Alternates shall carry out their duties as members of the Board of Governors without remuneration. The Fund, however, shall pay them appropriate expenses incurred in attending meetings.

8 The Board of Governors shall determine the remuneration to be paid to the members of the Board of Directors and their Alternates, as well as the salary and terms of the contract of service of the Director-General Chairman of the Board of Directors.

Article 20
Voting

1 For voting purposes at meetings of the Board of Governors, each member shall have two hundred votes, regardless of the number of shares it may hold, plus one additional vote for each share held.

2 Except as otherwise provided, all matters before the Board shall be decided by an absolute majority of votes.

Article 21
Director-General
Chairman of the
Board of Directors
and Staff

1 The Board of Governors shall appoint a Director-General to the Fund who is not a Governor or his Alternate, nor a Director or his Alternate. In case of a temporary absence of the Director-General, the Board of Governors shall appoint a replacement for him to act on his behalf during his absence.

2 The Director-General shall preside at the meetings of the Board of Directors. He shall have no vote, save in the event of an equal division, in which case he shall have a casting vote. He may be called to attend the

meetings of the Board of Governors and take part in its discussions, but shall not vote at such meetings.

3 The Director-General shall be the head of the Fund and shall be responsible for conducting all business under the supervision of the Board of Directors. He shall apply technical and administrative regulations within the Fund, and have the right to appoint and dismiss experts and staff in accordance with the regulations of the Fund.

4 The Director-General and staff owe their duty to the Fund. In the course of the conduct of business, they must not allow themselves to be influenced by any considerations other than the interest of the Fund, and they shall remain impartial in the discharge of their duties.

5 In appointing the staff, the Director-General shall pay due regard that positions be distributed to the extent possible amongst nationals of the Arab states and countries members of the Fund, provided that there shall be no departure from the principle of securing the required efficiency and expertise.

**Article 22
Board of
Directors**

1 The Board of Directors shall be charged with all the activities of the Fund in a general manner, and shall exercise the powers delegated to it by the Board of Governors.

2 The Board of Directors shall be composed of four full-time Directors elected by the Board of Governors from among Arab citizens of recognized experience and competence. They shall be elected for a term of two years renewable.

3 Members of the Board of Directors shall be elected as follows:

a Each Governor shall nominate as candidates one Director and one Alternate Director.

b The Board of Governors shall elect from among the candidates four Directors and four Alternate Directors, by a majority of votes.

    c Each Governor shall delegate to one of the elected Directors the number of votes he represents in the Board of Governors.

4 The Alternate Directors shall assist the Directors in their work and shall attend the meetings of the Board of Directors. An Alternate Director shall have the right to vote in the absence of the Director for whom he is acting.

5 The Directors and their Alternates shall continue in office until their successors are appointed. If the office of one of them becomes vacant for a maximum period of ninety days, the Governors whose votes were represented by the former Director shall select a successor for the remainder of the term, provided that such selection is approved by the Board of Governors. The successor shall be in the same position as his predecessor with respect to the number of votes which he represents.

6 Meetings of the Board of Directors shall be valid provided a quorum of two-thirds of the total votes is present.

7 Resolutions of the Board of Directors shall be adopted by an absolute majority of the votes cast unless otherwise provided.

Article 23
Loan Committees

1 Loan committees shall be formed to submit the necessary reports on the projects and the adequacy of the loans requested therefor.

2 Each committee shall include an expert selected by the Governor representing the member in whose territory the project is located, and one or more members of the technical staff of the Fund appointed by the Chairman of the Board of Directors.

Article 24
Reports and
Statements

The Fund shall issue an annual general report on its financial position. It may also issue a report on its activities with respect to the various projects as well as any other reports on the carrying out of its purposes. Such reports and statements shall be distributed to all members.

Article 25
Allocation of
Net Income

A 10 percent part of the annual net income of the Fund shall be allocated to the General Reserve. The Board of Governors may decide to allocate an additional amount to form a supplementary proportion to the number of shares held by them.

PART FIVE: WITHDRAWAL-SUSPENSION OF MEMBERSHIP SUSPENSION OF OPERATIONS

Article 26
Withdrawal of
Members

No member shall have the right to withdraw from the Fund before the expiry of five years of membership. Withdrawal shall be by way of submitting a notice in writing to the Head Office of the Fund, expressing the member's wish to withdraw. Withdrawal shall become effective on the date such notice is received.

Article 27
Suspension of
Membership

1 If a member fails to fulfill any of its obligations to the Fund, its membership may be suspended by decision of a majority of the Board of Governors. The member so suspended shall definitively cease to be a member one year from the date of suspension unless another decision is taken by a majority of votes to readmit the suspended member.
2 While under suspension a member shall not be entitled to exercise any rights under this Agreement, except the right of withdrawal.

Article 28
Rights and Obligations
of Governments
Ceasing to be
Members

1 When a Government ceases to be a member under the provisions of Articles 26 and 27, it shall remain liable for all its obligations to the Fund, so long as any part of the loans or guarantees contracted before it ceased to be a member are outstanding; but the former member shall cease to incur any liabilities with respect to new loans or guarantees entered into by the Fund and shall cease to share either in its income or expenses.
2 When a Government ceases to be a member, the Fund shall purchase the shares of such Government and settle its accounts. The

purchase price of the shares shall be the value shown by the books of the Fund or the paid up value, whichever is less.

3 The payment for shares purchased by the Fund under the preceding Paragraph shall be governed by the following conditions:

a The Fund shall withhold any amount due to the Government for its shares so long as such Government or any public or private organization or institution in its territory remains liable to the Fund. The Fund shall be entitled to lay hold on the amount withheld in settlement of outstanding loans and obligations. In any event, no amount due to a member shall be paid until at least six months after the date upon which it ceased to be a member.

b The Fund may pay to the Government for its shares a part of the amount withheld, in proportion to the rights recovered by the Fund.

c If any loss is sustanied by the Fund as a result of the operations undertaken by it under this Agreement and is still outstanding on the date when the Government ceased to be a member, and the amount of the loss exceeds the amount of the reserve provided to be set against such loss on the aforesaid date, then such Government shall be liable to repay upon demand the amount by which the purchase price of the said Government's shares by the Fund would have been reduced, if the loss had been taken into account when the purchase price was determined.

Article 29
Suspension of the
Operations of the
Fund and Liquidation
of its Assets

1 In an emergency the Board of Directors may temporarily suspend operations in respect of loans, guarantees and participation in projects. It shall convene the Board of Governors to an extraordinary meeting to consider the case and take a decision in this respect.

2 The Fund may suspend permanently its operations by decision of a majority of three-quarters of the votes of the Board of Governors. The Fund shall, following such a decision, forthwith cease all activities, except such operations and measures as are necessary to the realization, conservation and preservation of its assets and property. The Fund shall continue to exist, and all mutual rights and obligations between the Fund and its members under this Agreement shall remain standing until the final settlement of its obligations and distribution of its assets. During this time, no member may be suspended, nor may it withdraw, and no assets may be distributed to members except under the provisions of Part Five of this Agreement.

3 No distribution of the assets of the Fund may be made until all creditors' claims have been settled. Such assets shall be distributed proportionately to the shares held by each member. Distribution shall be effected in cash or other assets at such times and in such currencies as the Fund shall deem appropriate.

4 Any member receiving assets distributed by the Fund in accordance with the provisions of Part Five shall be subrogated to all the rights pertaining to such assets as the Fund enjoyed prior to their distribution.

PART SIX: LEGAL STATUS, IMMUNITIES AND PRIVILEGES

Article 30

1 The Fund shall possess juridical personality and, in particular, the capacity:

    a to contract;

    b to acquire immovable and movable property and to dispose of same;

    c to institute legal proceedings.

2 Actions shall be brought against the Fund in the courts having competent jurisdiction in the place where its Head Office is situated,

and may be brought against it as well in the
place where the dispute has arisen if the Fund
has a branch office or an agent authorized to
accept notice of process.

3 No actions shall be brought against the
Fund by members or persons acting for or
deriving claims from members.

4 All property and assets of the Fund shall,
wherever located and by whomsoever held in
the member countries, be immune from all
forms of provisional measures before the
delivery of final judgement against the Fund.

5 All property and assets of the Fund,
wherever located and by whomsoever held in
the member countries, shall be immune from
search, requisition, confiscation, expropriation, or any similar forms of compulsory
measures by an executive or legislative authority.

6 The papers, registers and documents of
the Fund, wherever located and by whomsoever held, shall be inviolable.

**Article 31
Freedom of Assets
from Restrictions**

All property and assets of the Fund, to the
extent necessary to carry out the operations
provided for in this Agreement and subject
to the provisions of this Agreement, shall be
free from all restrictions, regulations, con-
trols, and moratoria of any kind.

Article 32

Communications of the Fund shall be accorded by each member the same treatment
that it accords to the official communications
of other members.

**Article 33
Immunity from
Taxation in
Member Countries**

1 The Fund, its assets, property, income,
its operations and transactions provided for
in this Agreement, shall be immune from all
taxation and from all custom duties. The
Fund shall also be immune from the obligation of collection or payment of any tax or
duty.

2 Shares of the Fund shall be immune from
all taxes and duties when issued or circulated.

3 Bonds and securities issued by the Fund, as well as dividends, interest and commissions thereon and the like, by whomsoever held, shall be immune from taxation of any kind.

Article 34
Immunities and
Privileges of Officers
and Employees of
the Fund

1 Governors and their Alternates, Directors and their Alternates, officers and employees of the Fund shall enjoy the following:

    a Immunity from legal process with respect to acts performed by them in their official capacity;

    b Immunity from immigration restrictions, alien registration requirements and exchange control;

    c Travelling facilities;

    d Immunity from taxation regarding the salaries or remunerations paid to them by the Fund.

2 In addition to the privileges and immunities accorded to the Fund and its staff under this Agreement, the Board of Governors may determine any other privileges and immunities that it may deem necessary for the achievement of the purposes of the Fund.

Article 35
Amendment of
Provisions of the
Agreement

1 Any member, Governor, or Director, shall be entitled to propose amendments to this Agreement, by communicating the amendment proposal to the Chariman of the Board of Governors who shall bring the proposal before the Board at the earliest opportunity. If the proposal is approved by the Board, the Fund shall seek the opinion of all members on same. When three-fourths of the voting members have accepted the proposal, the Fund shall certify the amendment by formal communication addressed to all members. The amendment shall be registered with the Secretariat General.*

---

*The "Secretariat General" means the "Secretariat General of the League of Arab States".

2 Notwithstanding Paragraph 1 of this Article, acceptance by all members is required in the case of any amendment modifying:

    a The right to withdraw from the Fund provided in Article 26 hereof;

    b The limitation of the members' liability in respect of the unpaid portion of their shares as provided in Article 8 hereof;

    c An increase of the capital as authorized under Paragraph 3 of Article 6 hereof.

3 Amendments shall come into force for all members three months after the date of the formal communication issued by the Fund, unless a shorter period is fixed by the Board of Governors.

PART SEVEN: INTERPRETATION AND ARBITRATION

Article 36

1 It shall be within the competence of the Board of Governors to examine and settle all differences arising between any member and the Fund, or between the members themselves, regarding the interpretation of the provisions of this Agreement. The decision of the Board shall be final and binding.

2 Any member may appeal against the decisions of the Board of Directors interpreting any of the provisions of this Agreement to the Board of Governors who shall give a final and binding decision on the matter in dispute. The Fund, pending the decision of the Board of Governors, may act on the basis of the decision of the Board of Directors.

Article 37
Arbitration

Whenever a disagreement arises between the Fund and a State or a country which has ceased to be a member, or between the Fund and a member during the final liquidation of the Fund, any party may submit such disagreement to arbitration by a tribunal of three arbitrators, one appointed by the Fund, another by the second party, and the third arbitrator shall be selected by the two arbitrators.

In case the two arbitrators fail to agree on the selection of the third arbitrator, the Secretary General of the League of Arab States shall select one from among Arab jurists. The award of the arbitration tribunal shall be final and binding.

PART EIGHT: FINAL PROVISIONS

Article 38

Every Government shall become member of this Fund as of the date on which it shall deposit with the Secretariat General of the League of Arab States the instruments of ratification or accession.

Article 39
Ratification, Deposit and Accession

1 This Agreement shall be ratified by the signatory Arab states and countries, in accordance with their basic laws as early as possible. The instruments of ratification shall be deposited with the Secretariat General of the League of Arab States which shall make a record of the depositing of the instruments of ratification and to notify the Arab member states and countries thereof.
2 Arab states and countries which have not signed this Agreement may accede thereto, following the approval of the Board of Governors, by addressing a notification to the Secretary General of the League of Arab States who shall notify their accession to the Arab states and countries, members of the Fund.

Article 40

This Agreement shall come into force one month after the deposit of the instruments of ratification by states whose total subscription is not less than 45 percent of the capital stock provided for in Article 5 hereof.

Article 41

The Secretary General of the League of Arab States shall convene the first meeting of the Board of Governors.

IN WITNESS WHEREOF, the authorized delegates whose
names appear below have signed this Agreement on behalf
and in the name of their Governments.
Done in Cairo, on Thursday, 18th Safar 1388 H., 16th
May 1968, in a single document in Arabic to be kept with
the Secretariat General of the League of Arab States. A
certified true copy shall be handed to each signatory or
acceding state.

I. Official Documents and Reports

African Development Bank. 1970. Interim Report by the Board of Directors of the African Development. Abidjan: The African Development Bank.

Al-Atiqui, A. S. 1973. Address of the Chairman of the Board of Governors to the Second Annual Meeting of the Board of Governors. Kuwait: The Arab Fund for Economic and Social Development.

Arab Fund. 1972. Agreement Establishing the Arab Fund for Economic and Social Development. Kuwait: The Arab Fund for Economic and Social Development.

Government of Kuwait. Al-Kuwait Al-Yom 'Official Gazette'.

Inter-American Development Bank. 1974. 1973 Annual Report. Washington, D.C.: The Inter-American Development Bank.

Kuwait Fund. 1964. Second Annual Report. Kuwait: The Kuwait Fund for Arab Economic Development.

Kuwait Fund. 1965. Third Annual Report. Kuwait: The Kuwait Fund for Arab Economic Development.

Kuwait Fund. 1966. Fourth Annual Report. Kuwait: The Kuwait Fund for Arab Economic Development.

Kuwait Fund. 1967. Fifth Annual Report. Kuwait: The Kuwait Fund for Arab Economic Development.

Kuwait Fund. 1968. Sixth Annual Report. Kuwait: The Kuwait Fund for Arab Economic Development.

Kuwait Fund. 1969. Seventh Annual Report. Kuwait: The Kuwait Fund for Arab Economic Development.

Kuwait Fund. 1970. Eighth Annual Report. Kuwait: The Kuwait Fund for Arab Economic Development.

Kuwait Fund. 1971. Ninth Annual Report. Kuwait: The Kuwait Fund for Arab Economic Development.

Kuwait Fund. 1972. Tenth Annual Report. Kuwait: The Kuwait Fund for Arab Economic Development.

Kuwait Fund. 1973. Eleventh Annual Report. Kuwait: The Kuwait Fund for Arab Economic Development.

Kuwait Fund. 1974. Basic Information. Kuwait: The Kuwait Fund for Arab Economic Development.

II. Newspapers

As-Siassa 'Politics'. A Kuwait Daily.

III. Books

Buckley, W. 1967. Sociology and Modern Systems Theory. Englewood
    Cliffs, N.J.: Prentice-Hall.

Cohen, P. S. 1968. Modern Social Theory. New York: Basic Books.

Dexter, L. A. 1970. Elite and Specialized Interviewing. Evanston,
    Ill.: Northwestern University Press.

Dickson, H. R. P. 1956. Kuwait and Her Neighbours. London: George
    Allen & Unwin.

Easton, D. 1953. The Political System: An Inquiry into the State of
    Political Science. New York: Knopf.

El-Mallakh, R. 1968. Economic Development and Regional Coopera-
    tion: Kuwait. Chicago: University of Chicago Press.

Etzioni, A. 1961. A Comparative Analysis of Complex Organizations:
    On Power, Involvement, and their Correlates. New York: The
    Free Press.

Freeth, Z. 1972. A New Look at Kuwait. London: George Allen &
    Unwin.

Holden, D. 1966. Farewell to Arabia. New York: Walker and Com-
    pany.

Ilchman, W. F. and N. Uphoff. 1969. The Political Economy of
    Change. Berkeley: University of California Press.

Ismael, T. Y. 1974. The Middle East in World Politics: A Study in
    Contemporary International Relations. Syracuse, N.Y.: Syra-
    cuse University Press.

LaPorte, T. R. 1971. "The Recovery of Relevance in the Study of
    Public Organizations," in F. Marini (ed.) Toward a New Public
    Administration: The Minnowbrook Perspective. Scranton, Calif.:
    Chandler Publishing Co.

Mason, E. D. and R. E. Asher. 1973. The World Bank Since Bretton-
    Woods. Washington, D. C.: The Brookings Institution.

Mikesell, R. 1966. Public International Lending for Development.
    New York: Random House.

Mouzelis, N. P. 1969. Organization and Bureaucracy: An Analysis
    of Modern Theories. Chicago: Aldine.

Nutting, A. 1964. The Arabs: A Narrative History from Mohammed
    to the Present. New York: Clarkson N. Potter, Inc.

Pearson, L. 1969. Partners in Development: Report of the Commis-
    sion on International Development. New York: Praeger.

Price, J. L. 1968. Organizational Effectiveness: An Inventory of
    Propositions. Homewood, Ill.: Irwin.

Selltiz, C. et al. 1959. Research Methods in Social Relations. New
    York: Holt, Rinehart and Winston.

Silverman, D. 1970. The Theory of Organizations. London: Heine-
    mann.

Stephens, R. 1973. The Arabs' New Frontier. London: Temple Smith.
Thompson, J. D. 1967. Organizations in Action. New York: McGraw-
    Hill.
Thompson, J. D., P. B. Hammond et al. 1959. Comparative Studies
    in Administration. Pittsburgh: University of Pittsburgh Press.
Wall, D. 1973. The Charity of Nations: The Political Economy of
    Foreign Aid. New York: Basic Books.
Wamsley, G. and M. Zald. 1973. The Political Economy of Public
    Organizations. Lexington, Mass.: D. C. Heath.
White, J. L. 1972. Regional Development Banks: The African, Asian
    and Inter-American Development Banks. New York: Praeger.
    _____. 1974. Promotion of Economic Integration Through Devel-
    opment Finance Institutions: Three Case Studies. Geneva:
    UNCTAD Publications (TAD/EI/MFI/R.2).
Winder, R. B. 1965. Saudi Arabia in the Nineteenth Century. New
    York: St. Martin's Press.
Winstone, H. V. F. and Z. Freeth. 1972. Kuwait: Prospect and
    Reality. New York: Crane, Russak and Co.

IV. Articles and Papers

Al-Awadi, Y. 1971. Kuwait Official Foreign Aid: Channels and Per-
    spectives. Kuwait: Kuwait Institute of Economic and Social
    Planning in the Middle East.
Al-Hamad, A. Y. 1971. The Kuwait Fund. Kuwait: The Kuwait Fund
    for Arab Economic Development (in Arabic).
    _____. 1972. Building Up Development-oriented Institutions in
    the Arab Countries. Kuwait: The Kuwait Fund for Arab Economic
    Development.
    _____. 1973a. Arab Funds and International Economic Cooperation.
    Kuwait: The Kuwait Fund for Arab Economic Development.
    _____. 1973b. Arab Capital and International Finance. Kuwait:
    The Kuwait Fund for Arab Economic Development.
    _____. 1974. Bilateral Development Aid: The View from the
    Kuwait Fund. Kuwait: The Kuwait Fund for Arab Economic
    Development.
Bloch, H. S. 1968. "Regional development financing." International
    Organization 22 (Winter): 182-203.
Bowey, A. M. 1972. "Approaches to organization theory." Social
    Science Information 11 (December): 109-28.
Caporaso, J. A. 1971. "Theory and method in the study of international
    integration." International Organization 25 (Spring): 228-63.
Dalkey, N. and O. Helmer. 1963. "An experimental application of the
    Delphi Method to use of experts." Management Science 9 (April):
    458-67.

Dawe, A. 1970. "The two sociologies." British Journal of Sociology
    21 (June): 207-18.
Dessouki, A. E. 1973. "Arab intellectuals and Al-Nakba: the search
    for fundamentalism." Middle Eastern Studies 9 (May): 187-96.
El-Mallakh, R. 1974. "The absorptive capacity of Arab economies."
    Paper presented to the Seminar on Investment Policies of Arab
    Oil-Producing Countries. Kuwait, 24-28 February.
Ghali, M. B. 1974. "The place of Egyptian identity in Arab nation-
    alism." As-Siassa Ad-Dawlia 'International Politics' 10 (April):
    278-97 (in Arabic).
Hass, E. 1970. "The study of regional integration: reflections on the
    joy and anguish of pretheorizing." International Organization
    24 (Autumn): 607-46.
Hass, M. 1974. "Asian development bank." International Organization
    28 (Spring): 281-96.
Ilchman, W. F. 1971. "Comparative public administration and 'con-
    ventional wisdom.'" Beverly Hills: Sage Professional Papers
    in Comparative Politics.
Mabro, R. and E. Monroe. 1974. "Arab wealth from oil: the prob-
    lems of its investment." International Affairs 50 (January): 15-
    27.
Mohr, L. 1973. "The concept of organizational goal." The American
    Political Science Review 67 (June): 470-80.
Perrow, C. 1961. "The analysis of goals in complex organizations."
    American Sociological Review 26 (December): 854-65.
Rustow, D. 1974. "Who won the Yom Kippur and oil wars." Foreign
    Policy 17 (Winter): 166-75.
Shehab, F. 1964. "Kuwait: a super affluent society." Foreign Affairs
    42 (April): 461-74.
Shihata, I. 1973. The Kuwait Fund for Arab Economic Development:
    A Legal Analysis. Kuwait: The Kuwait Fund for Arab Economic
    Development.
_____. 1974a. Arab Investment-Guarantee Corporation: Its Role
    in Directing the Movement of Arab Investments. Kuwait: The
    Kuwait Fund for Arab Economic Development (in Arabic).
_____. 1974b. "The oil wealth facing Arab development problems."
    As-Siassa Ad-Dawlia 'International Politics' 10 (April): 26-48
    (in Arabic).
Singh, M. 1970. "Regional development banks." International Concili-
    ation 576 (January).

Abu-Dhabi, 65
Abu-Dhabi Fund for Arab Economic and Social Development, 95, 96
action approach (theory), 13-14, 15, 99-100
African Development Bank, 54, 60, 61
Agency for International Development (USAID) (United States), 19-20, 54-55, 60
Algeria, 57, 70
Al-Hamad, 5-6, 14-15, 21-22, 24, 27, 28, 32, 38, 39, 40-41, 45, 58
Arab Fund for Economic and Social Development, 19, 37, 57-58, 79, 83, 101; board of directors, 86, 96; board of governors, 85-86, 93, 95, 96; decision making in, 92-93; interest rates on loans, 94; membership, 84; president, 86-87, 93, 94
Arab League, 4, 11, 19, 22, 52, 58
Arab nationalism, 4, 78-79
Arab Organization for Management Development, 52
Arab States, defined 11
Arab unity, 67-68
Asian Development Bank, 54, 60, 61

Bahrain, 11, 22-23, 25, 57, 73, 84
board of directors (Kuwait Fund), 7-8, 10, 22-24, 37
Britain, 2-5

China, 70, 72
Confederation of Arab Labor Unions, 19

decision making, 15, 19, 33-34, 42, 66, 99; in the Arab Fund, 92-93; in the Kuwait Fund, 33-37; collegial structure of, 35, 40-41; Thompson's matrix of, 35
development banks, 36-37; African Development Bank, 54, 60, 61; Asian Development Bank, 54, 60, 61; Inter-American Development Bank (IDB), 54, 60, 61, 63
disbursements, 47-48, 61, 62-63

effectiveness, 13-14, 19, 20, 34-35, 42, 61-62, 100; appraisal of Kuwait Fund, 98-99; defined, 16
Egypt, 4, 12, 30, 71, 73, 78, 84
Etzioni, A., 15

General Authority for South Arabian and Gulf States, 26
Germany, 3

IBRD (see, World Bank)
Industrial Development Centre for the Arab States (IDCAS), 52
Inter-American Development Bank (IDB), 54, 60, 61, 63
Inter-Arab Investment Guarantee Corporation, 57-59
interest rates: on African Development Bank loans, 54; on

Arab Fund loans, 94; on
Asian Development Bank
loans, 54; on Inter-American
Development Bank loans, 54;
on Kuwait Fund loans, 53-54;
on World Bank loans, 54
International Monetary Fund
(IMF), 57, 89, 92, 93
Iraq, 4-5, 25, 30, 71, 84
Islam, 68; Islamic fundamen-
talism, 71
Israel, 64, 65, 68

Japan, 72
Jordan, 22, 84

Khartoum conference 1967, 22
Koran, 29
Kuwait, 14, 19, 21-22, 25-26,
28, 33-34, 40, 44, 48, 49-
50, 56-57, 60-61, 65, 67,
70, 72, 81-82, 84, 85-86,
87, 91-92, 98, 100; Arab
policy of, 11; area, 3; discovery of oil in, 4; independence, 4, 18; political
system, 70; relations with
Britain 1-5; relations with
Ottoman Empire, 2; value of
currency in U.S. dollars, 9
Kuwait Investment Company
(KIC), 32

Lebanon, 12, 22, 25, 30, 57,
70, 71, 72, 81, 84
Libya, 84

Malaysia, 100
Mikesell, R., 46, 53
Mohr, L., 16-17
Morocco, 12, 71, 73, 84

October 1973 War, 67, 79
oil, 3-4, 21, 32, 52, 64-65, 67,
79-80, 100; discovery in

Kuwait, 4; investment in oil
industry, 80
Organization of Petroleum Exporting Countries (OPEC), 79
organization theory, 99-100
Ottoman Empire, 2

Pearson Report, 48-49
Perrow, C., 16, 18
Philippines, 100
political ideology, 63, 68, 71
portfolio investment, 28, 61
Price, J., 99
professional staff (Kuwait Fund),
9-10, 14-15
program lending, 46-48
project appraisal, 49, 92
project lending; in the Arab Fund,
94-95; in Kuwait Fund, 46-48,
51
project selection, 51

Qatar, 84

Soviet Union, 70, 72
Sudan, 25, 30, 57, 78
Syria, 4, 25, 30, 71, 78, 81, 84,
94

technical assistance, 34, 46, 57;
types of, 55
Thailand, 100
Thompson, J. D., 15-16, 18, 33,
35
"tied" loans, 55
Tunisia, 12, 25, 71, 84, 94

United Nations, 5, 92
United States, 19, 48, 70, 71, 72
Uqair Conference, 3

White, J., 50, 51
World Bank, 12-13, 47, 49-51,
53, 55, 57, 84, 89, 93-94,
98; interest rates on loans, 54

Yemen (North), 10, 25, 30, 57, 84

Yemen (South), 25, 26, 84, 94
Yugoslavia, 70

ABOUT THE AUTHOR

SOLIMAN DEMIR is a Research Associate at the United Nations Institute for Training and Research (UNITAR). He previously worked in a research capacity at the National Bank of Egypt, the National Center for Social Research, and the National Institute of Management Development in Egypt.

Dr. Demir has published articles on politics, economics, and administration of development in such journals as Management Quarterly, International Politics Quarterly, and Economist Al-Ahram in Egypt.

Dr. Demir holds B.S. and M.S. degrees from Cairo University, an M.A. from the American University of Beirut, and a Ph.D. from the University of Pittsburgh.

ARAB OIL: Impact on Arab Nations and Global Implications
edited by Naiem A. Sherbiny
and Mark A. Tessler

MULTILATERAL AND BILATERAL AID: A Comparative Analysis
of Aid Criteria
William Loehr and Satish Raichur

DEVELOPMENT OF THE IRANIAN OIL INDUSTRY: International
and Domestic Aspects
Fereidun Fesharaki

THE SAUDI ARABIAN ECONOMY
Ramon Knauerhase

DEVELOPMENT WITHOUT DEPENDENCE
Pierre Uri